INTERPRETING POLICY IN REAL CLASSROOMS

Case Studies of State Reform and Teacher Practice

INTERPRETING POLICY IN REAL CLASSROOMS

Case Studies of State Reform and Teacher Practice

Nancy E. Jennings

FOREWORD BY DAVID K. COHEN

Teachers College, Columbia University
New York and London

Published by Teachers College Press, 1234 Amsterdam Avenue, New York, NY 10027

Copyright © 1996 by Teachers College, Columbia University

Library of Congress Cataloging-in-Publication Data

Jennings, Nancy E.
    Interpreting policy in real classrooms : case studies of state
reform and teacher practice / Nancy E. Jennings.
        p.   cm.
    Includes bibliographical references and index.
    ISBN 0-8077-3491-8 (cloth : alk. paper).—ISBN 0-8077-3490-X
(pbk. : alk. paper)
    1. Reading—Michigan—Case studies.   2. Cognitive learning—
Michigan—Case studies.   3. Education—Standards—Michigan.
4. Educational change—Michigan—Case studies.   I. Title.
LB1050.42.J46   1996
372.4—dc20   95-44895

ISBN 0-8077-3490-X (paper)
ISBN 0-8077-3491-8 (cloth)
Printed on acid-free paper
Manufactured in the United States of America
03 02 01 00 99 98 97 96   8 7 6 5 4 3 2 1

Contents

Foreword

The last decade witnessed remarkable developments in American education. Beginning with the California mathematics framework in 1985, states began to devise new goals and standards that were designed to press teaching and learning toward more substantial and demanding work. This was a new generation of education policies, for they focused much more explicitly and ambitiously on instruction than ever before. As the state policies multiplied they gained support from President Bush's announcement of national education goals in a meeting with the governors at Charlottesville, from the work of the National Education Goals Panel that was formed in the wake of the Charlottesville education summit, and from the efforts of business and civic leaders to mobilize support for the proposed reforms. The state and national efforts were hopeful and exciting, for they held out the promise of much more engaging work for children and much more challenging careers for teachers. What had begun as a modest trickle of new ideas in the mid-1980s could fairly be called a movement by the early 1990s.

But the state reforms faced one enormous problem. Precisely because they proposed such sweeping instructional changes, the new policies could not succeed unless education professionals learned to think and act in quite unfamiliar ways. Most teachers and administrators would not only have to learn much more about academic subjects, instruction, and learning, but they also would have to learn to work much differently. In fact, the reforms embody a paradox. Teachers and other education professionals are the chief problem, because it is their inexperience and lack of knowledge that stand in the way of better instruction for children. But teachers and other education professionals also are the chief solution to the problem, for it is difficult to imagine how most students' learning could be improved unless educators become the agents of improvement.

Learning would seem to be the solution to this problem—that is, the new policies would only work if teachers and other education professionals learned a great deal and remade their practice. Learning is of course an element of all policies—even the 55 MPH speed limit entailed that drivers learn new ideas, habits, and procedures. But learning looms much larger in the new instructional policies because they call on educators to perform in ways with which only a few have much experience. State and federal policymakers nearly always depend on local teachers, social workers, or civil servants to carry out their policies, and to learn things en route. But in this case state education policymakers greatly expanded the learning that they would depend on teachers to undertake, because the reforms proposed to expand the depth and difficulty of instruction far beyond most teachers' experience and knowledge.

Hence the new policies would have to be deeply educational for educators if they were to have any hope of being effective. Policy analysts regularly worry about the effects that policy has on such things as school budgets or students' learning, but these policies opened up a relatively unfamiliar domain of effects, namely, on professionals' learning. Professor Jennings' book begins to explore that terrain. She spent several years investigating teachers' response to a more ambitious reading policy that was adopted by the Michigan Department of Education in the mid-1980s. After sketching the policy and briefly summarizing state officials' efforts to inform teachers about it, Professor Jennings focuses most of her attention in this book on what three teachers did and did not learn in the course of Michigan's effort to improve the reading instruction. The very shape of the book thus makes one of its chief arguments, namely, that teachers' learning is a central element in the enactment and success of the new policies designed to improve students' learning.

This is an important book in part because it suggests an entire world of novel issues with which practitioners and policymakers are trying to deal as they pursue efforts to improve instruction. I am not an entirely dispassionate observer—Professor Jennings and I have been colleagues in a larger study of which this work is one part—but when readers consider a few of the issues that this book opens up, I think they will agree with my assessment.

To begin with, cognitive scientists and other students of learning now depict learners as sense makers, and they portray the mind as active and interpretive in its encounters with experience. They see the mind as an active contributor to experience rather than as its passive product. These researchers further explain that one reason minds' actions and interpretations differ is that their previous experience differs. The authors of the new Michigan reading policy adopted that doctrine, and exhorted teachers to take students' prior knowledge and experience into account as they devised lessons or listened to students' comments on a story. They reasoned that teachers then would be better able to adapt lessons to students' thinking, and to understand students' thinking about their reading. But what's sauce for the goose may be sauce for the gander: If teachers are learners from policy, and if their knowledge and experience vary one from another like other learners', then their readings of new policies also could be expected to differ widely. Professor Jennings' account of the great differences among three Michigan teachers highlights that point, and her study leaves us with a crucial question for the new policies: How can we square the constructivist idea that as teachers make sense of and learn from instructional policies they will make different sense of them, with the recognition that policy typically seeks general if not uniform results?

A second issue begins with the recognition that learning often entails teaching, especially when learners are being asked to do something as unfamiliar as the revised reading policy invited teachers to do. Few would propose to teach algebra by telling students to learn it, giving them a brief book on the subject, and walking away. The Michigan State Department of Education staff recognized that teaching would be in order, and once the new policy was announced staffers launched an effort to teach teachers about the new ideas and practices. But as Professor Jennings shows, that state effort was very modest when compared with the scope and scale of the learning that reformers proposed for teachers—not because state staffers were malicious or ignorant, but because they had pitifully small resources to deploy in their efforts to improve education. The state department was small, it employed only one reading specialist to serve more than five hundred school districts in a state roughly the size of New England, and the state agency had neither money nor other staff capability to help tens of thousands of teachers to learn. Professor Jennings' book focuses on this problem in three small worlds, for her case studies reveal the rather modest opportunities that the three teachers had to learn about the new policy. But in doing so she opens up a large question: New policies that propose extensive learning for teachers exist in state and local school systems that have little capacity for professional education; what can reasonably be expected from such an arrangement?

A third issue grows out of one of Professor Jennings' central conclusions. She argues that ". . . the worth of a policy is in what teachers learn from it." That seems entirely reasonable if the policy in question requires that educators learn a great deal in order to respond constructively. But it could seem entirely unreasonable to state or federal legislators, who often see policy as a matter of "sending a message" rather than offering a full-service treatment. One distinctive feature of the period that Professor Jennings studied was a combination of increasing ambitions for results of schooling and decreasing willingness to invest in the enterprise. What will be the result of state and national efforts to maintain or raise educational standards if they are not accompanied by parallel efforts to improve educators' capacities to deliver the goods?

Professor Jennings does not offer simple answers to these and other issues. But in exploring them she suggests some of the new dimensions that the recent school reform movement has opened up, in both policy and policy analysis. Her thoughtful comments on the connections and disconnections between state policy and classroom practice will be useful to many readers.

David K. Cohen
University of Michigan

Acknowledgments

I have been very lucky to have received intellectual and emotional support from my teachers, my colleagues, my friends, and my family. I would like to thank some of them here, but only after saying that my acknowledgment of thanks, a common thing for authors to do, in no way reflects the very uncommon gifts I know they have given me.

First, the teachers—Catherine Price, Tom Fielder, and Kate Stern—put up with my presence in their classrooms over a number of years, as well as my endless questions. These people allowed me into their classrooms and their lives. I am extremely grateful to them not only for the accommodations they made, but for confirming once again for me the goodness of people who teach. Even when I questioned their views and practices, I was always struck by how seriously they took the responsibility of educating children.

Next, I acknowledge the Educational Policy and Practice Study out of which this book grew, whose principal investigators are Deborah Lowenberg Ball, David K. Cohen, Penelope Peterson, and Suzanne Wilson. Other researchers on the project are Peggy Aiken, Carol Barnes, Jennifer Borman, Jim Bowker, Daniel Chazan, Pamela Geist, S. G. Grant, Ruth Heaton, Nancy Knapp, Susan Luks, Steve Mattson, Sue Poppink, Richard Prawat, Jeremy Price, Ralph Putnam, Janine Remillard, Angela Shojgreen-Downer, and James Spillane, Sarah Theule-Lubienski, and Karl Wheatley. All of these people have helped me greatly. They have listened to long discussions of my field notes, read interviews, and engaged in many conversations about ideas related to policy and practice. Secretaries for the project—Cindy Casey, Stephanie Grant, Patti Havercamp, and Lisa Roy—helped me keep track of the data. I am particularly indebted to David Cohen, S. G. Grant, and Jim Spillane for their help in thinking about these issues. The four of us have been working for the last few years to analyze the Michigan reading policy. My thinking about reading policy and classroom practices has grown greatly because of our work together. The views expressed in this book, though, are my own and not necessarily shared by the Grantors nor other researchers on the project.

The Educational Policy and Practice Study has been supported in part by grants from the Pew Charitable Trust (Grant No. 91-04343-000), Carnegie Corporation of New York (Grant No. B 5638), the National Science Foundation (Grant No. ESI-9153834), the Consortium for Policy Research in Education (CPRE), the National Center for Research on Teacher Leaning (NCRTL) and Michigan State University. CPRE and NCRTL are funded by grants from the U.S. Department of Education, Office of Educational Research and Improvement (Grant No. OERI-G-00869001 and No. OERI-R-117G10011-94).

In addition to my colleagues on the research project, Helen Featherstone and G. Williamson McDiarmid read countless drafts of this work and kept their sanity and mine through all of them. More recently Penny Martin and Sally MacKenzie, my colleagues at Bowdoin College, saw me through the final stages of this work.

Finally, I'd like to thank my family. My parents who have never failed to be supportive of me and delighted by my accomplishments. My daughters, Emily and Alice, who help me remember what schools are really for and for whom they exist. My husband, Gene Wiemers, who has been helpful in too many ways to list. We have been together for twenty-five years and lived through many things—two children, two dissertations, a few houses, too many pets. I cherish our life together.

INTERPRETING POLICY IN REAL CLASSROOMS

Case Studies of State Reform and Teacher Practice

Introduction

Reading has been a centerpiece in recent efforts to push ambitious approaches to teaching and learning. In the early 1980s, reading researchers began to shift the focus of their work away from views of reading that emphasized discrete skills and toward views that emphasized reading comprehension and the cognitive processes of reading (Anderson, Hiebert, Scott, & Wilkinson, 1985; Willinsky, 1989). State policymakers followed suit, developing policies that concentrated on how readers construct meaning of text and on the texts readers read (e.g., California State Department of Education, 1987; Michigan State Board of Education, 1985). Michigan policymakers were among the first to call for changes in reading instruction.

Before the reform effort, in the typical Michigan classroom, as elsewhere in the country, reading focused on isolated skills. Michigan's definition of reading described it as "the process of transforming the visual representation of language into meaning." During reading instruction, teachers helped students learn word-attack skills by reading controlled pieces of text from basal readers and by answering short-response questions in the accompanying workbooks. After students acquired enough necessary skills, they could begin to extract meaning from texts (Durkin, 1978–1979; Michigan Reading Association [MRA], 1984).

In the early 1980s, reading researchers were beginning to recast reading instruction, but many teachers were not. Armed with a new Ph.D. in reading and fully versed in current thinking about reading, Michigan's state reading consultant sought to reduce the discrepancy between research and practice. Joining her in this effort was a small group of like-minded researchers and practitioners in the state who began to elicit additional support from others—reading teachers, university researchers, and members of the Michigan Reading Association (MRA). This small group of reformers challenged local school districts to revise their reading curricula along lines suggested by the most current reading research. They rewrote the state definition of reading and began work on revised state goals and objectives for reading. When they had acquired enough support for the changes they envisioned from educators around the state, the reformers asked the State Board of Education to approve the revised reading definition, which the board did in 1985.

The new definition described reading as a "process of constructing meaning through the dynamic interaction among: the reader's existing knowledge, the information suggested by the written language, and the context of the reading situation" (Michigan State Department of Education, 1987, p. 1; MRA, 1984). The change in definition was significant. Whereas the old definition concentrated on skills, the new one highlighted both the readers' role in constructing meaning of text and the ways in which the purpose and context of the reading experience shape readers' textual interpretations. Whereas the old definition implied a consistent and solitary meaning of text, the new one left open the possibility of readers' constructing various meanings of the same text. Considerations of the reader and context were new for teachers; so was the idea of multiple meanings of texts. These new ideas implied big changes in classroom practices. Teachers would have to find out more about their students' prior understandings in order to understand how they were comprehending text. They would also have to think about reasons for reading particular texts. Teachers would have to find new ways to assess student comprehension of text if more than one correct interpretation of text was possible.

Perhaps the biggest change in the definition was the role skill instruction should play in reading. In a position paper written around the time of state approval of the definition, MRA (1984) leaders wrote:

> The existing definition implies the existence of a discrete set of skills that, when mastered, add up to reading. In contrast, the new definition implies that the goal of instruction is to develop in students the ability to apply reading skills and strategies. . . . Skill mastery is a means to this end, not an end in itself. (p. 2)

For many teachers whose reading practice focused on skill instruction, the notion that skills were merely a means to an end, and that application of skills and comprehension should be the focus of reading, implied radical changes.

Michigan's reformers recognized that the changes they were advocating would require them to do more than merely change the state's definition of reading and write new goals and objectives. If their ideas were going to influence classroom practice, the reformers would have to help teachers learn about new concepts of reading and reading practice. Reformers approached the issue of teaching about the policy with the same fervor that they tackled changing the state definition. They designed a series of state-sponsored conferences on the policy for teachers to attend. For meetings of this sort, these conferences were very well attended and the State Department of Education continued to sponsor them for a number of years. In addition, the State Department of Education designed materials that could be used by staff developers in districts to teach teachers who had not attended state conferences about the new reading policy. These materials included scripts of conference sessions and copies of transparencies used in the state workshops. The state reading consultant referred to these materials as ways to help other practitioners "do what I do" so that the word of reading reform could be spread throughout the state.

Reformers also undertook the revision of the state mandated assessment of reading, the Michigan Educational Assessment Program (MEAP), so that it would reflect the new vision. Many reformers talked about the revision of the MEAP as a key piece of their work. Since the late 1960s, when the MEAP was first administered, test scores had become increasingly more important to practitioners, particularly district superintendents. Test scores were often reported in newspapers, and districts and schools were often held accountable by the public for the results. Without some changes in the MEAP, policymakers feared that administrators and teachers would not attend to their new ideas. As long as the reading MEAP tested discrete skills, teachers would have reasons to teach them. One policymaker stated that the MEAP, like all state assessments, "drives instruction" so that the reformers' goal was to have the MEAP drive instruction in the new ways they envisioned. The new MEAP test was first given statewide in 1989, to students in grades 4, 7, and 10. As reformers predicted, test scores declined in most districts and as a result many practitioners took a new interest in what reformers were saying about reading and attempted to institute changes in classroom practices.

As with the writing of the definition, state policymakers involved practitioners across the state in these and other efforts to implement the new reading policy. Practitioners were asked to help write questions for the new MEAP test and to review sample items. Others served on the committees that reviewed new objectives and goals. The state reading consultant formed the Curriculum Review Committee (CRC) to develop new ideas about classroom practices that would foster the kind of reading instruction envisioned in the new definition. She placed on this committee practitioners from around the state who she knew were already committed to making changes in reading. CRC members helped design the state conferences and were instrumental in bringing the ideas and materials from the conferences to districts around the state. All of these efforts resulted in the reading reform's becoming commonplace in practitioners' conversations about reading. Five years after the reading definition was approved by the state board, one of the definition's writers said that she doubted there was a teacher in the state who had not at least heard of the new reading policy.

Within a short period of time, then, state reformers asked Michigan teachers to change radically the ways in which they thought about and taught reading. Reading skills were to be taught as a means to the end of comprehension. Comprehension of text was now a dynamic process shaped by both the reader and the context of reading. Because this policy was about changing practice, teachers had to figure out what these ideas meant and what they implied for their classrooms. What follows are stories of three teachers' reading practices. Their stories include the changes they have made in light of the new policy as well as the changes they have not made. The stories also include the teachers' learning from and about the policy and their interpretations of what they learned.

METHODS OF STUDY

To gather the information for this book, I spent a long time talking with teachers about their literacy practices and observing them teach. The interviews I did with teachers provided me opportunities to listen to their reconstructions of their own learning, as well to listen to many other thoughts about teaching, reading, students, and schools. In the text that follows, all quotations not otherwise attributed came from these interviews. Pseudonyms are used for all teacher and administrator names in this book. Pseudonyms are used as well for city, school, and district names.

Looking at learning is difficult because learning is a very complex and personal event that occurs within an individual in a particular context and time. Even the learners themselves cannot often articulate exactly what they are thinking, what has influenced their thinking, and when they actually can say they have "learned" something. In this study, I attempt to do something that may be even more complex, and that is to ask teachers to reconstruct their own learning that occurred in the past—learning that may in some ways have shaped their current thinking and practice. This means that I had to ask teachers to step outside their current context and time to remember what they might have been thinking and doing at the time they first learned from and about the policy. A few times in the interviews, it was clear that stepping outside was hard for the teachers to do— to separate themselves from what they know/think/believe to remember what they knew/thought/believed at the time they first heard about the policy and then to think forward from that time to their current context. Interviewing teachers many times over an extended period of time—four years in some cases—helped us work on this difficulty and develop what seems like a robust and textured reconstruction of their learning.

Observations conducted as the teachers put the "policy" into practice helped me put in context much of what they told me. The teachers I observed learned in the particular contexts in which their learning played out—their classrooms, districts, school communities. Their learning was shaped by these contexts as well as by who they were and what they brought to their learning. Bruner (1990) suggests that what one does "reveals what one thinks, feels, or believes" because "saying and doing represent a functionally inseparable unit" (p. 19). In this study, what teachers did in their classrooms helped me understand the meaning they gave to terms they used, terms such as "whole language," "literature-based instruction," "integrated instruction." Because I observed teachers many times over a number of years (again, in some cases as long as four years), I was able to change the focus of my subsequent observations to fit new areas of interest that arose out of the interviews and previous observations. In this way, the interviews and observations informed one another and helped me better understand how these teachers thought and acted about the policy and about their reading practices.

My ability to figure out what the issues were—in other words, what I should look for and ask—improved as I got to know the teachers better and understood more about the environments in which they worked. Ethnographers write about the importance of placing oneself in the worlds of the people one is studying to understand their frames of reference (Blumer, 1976; Bogdan & Biklen, 1982). Observing these teachers work with their students in their classrooms, talking to others in their schools, hanging out in the teachers' lounges, talking to administrators in their districts, and exploring the communities in which their schools were located helped me develop a better sense of their frames of references and of the experiences and opportunities that may be important to them.

At the core of this study are cases of three teachers who learned, interpreted, and implemented the reading policy in different ways. By looking at the relationships among interpretation, learning, and implementation through stories of these teachers' thinking and practices, I hope to keep intact as much as possible the complexities that they faced as they attempted to do their best to learn, interpret, and implement policy. Coles (1989) writes: "We owe it to each other to respect our stories and learn from them" (p. 30). Through stories of these teachers' efforts in the often messy context in which they occurred, I tried to learn more about what it means for teachers to learn from policies and to analyze how that plays out in their lives as teachers.

CHAPTER 1

Learning to Teach Reading

It was very frightening when it first came out because, you know, they would go over the new definition and show us all of those graphs and charts. And I went, "Oh no! I've been doing it wrong all these years." I think all teachers go through this when they are given new information to learn.

T. Fielder

When we met, Tom Fielder had been teaching second-graders to read for several years. He had always taught reading in what would be considered "traditional" ways. Students learned to read by first learning phonics and sight words. They read from basal readers and answered questions about the text in workbooks that accompany the basals. Mr. Fielder said he felt successful teaching that way. His students did well on standardized tests for reading, and the third-grade teachers in his building were pleased to get Mr. Fielder's students. They knew his students came well prepared in the basics.

In the mid-1980s Mr. Fielder heard that the state of Michigan was revising its definition of reading and was setting new goals and objectives for reading instruction. Rumors of this change made him quite anxious. He felt successful in teaching children to read and liked the way he did it. He knew his practices were similar to those of many teachers in the state, but he also knew that there were more innovative ideas about teaching reading that some teachers, in his building and elsewhere, were following. When the new definition was officially announced in 1985, it represented a shift away from the modal practices and thinking with which Mr. Fielder identified. The definition stated: "Reading is the process of constructing meaning through dynamic interaction among the reader, the text, and the context of the reading situation" (MRA, 1984). Mr. Fielder, like many educators across the state, said he was not sure what the definition meant and what its implications were for reading practices. The definition focused on constructing meaning from text and called reading a dynamic process.

It brought to the fore the reader's role in the reading process and the context or purposes of reading. But what did these ideas mean for students learning to read in classrooms? What different things would Mr. Fielder have to do to teach in a way compatible with this definition? Mr. Fielder did not know the answers to these questions. Given the way he thought about reading instruction and the way he taught reading, he said he knew he would have a lot to learn.

THE READING POLICY: A SHIFT IN FOCUS

From the very beginning, state policymakers also knew that teachers would have to learn new things in order to implement the changes in reading practice envisioned by the policy. One of the writers of the policy remarked:

> One of the issues that became very clear about this whole process is that change was occurring because of this knowledge and I think in the past knowledge has not been a primary factor. . . . It's not gimmicks. It's not things that are going to be kind of glitzy. It's knowledge.

Prior to the introduction of the policy, reading instruction in most classrooms in the state looked a lot like Mr. Fielder's. Students spent much of their instructional time being drilled on isolated skills or answering literal questions in reading workbooks. Students read short passages in basal readers and little time was devoted to comprehension of text (Durkin, 1978-1979; MRA, 1987). These practices were consistent with state policy at the time. Reading was defined by the state as a series of discrete, hierarchically ordered skills that had to be learned before readers could comprehend a text. The state reading test, the Michigan Educational Assessment Program (MEAP), measured how well students mastered the isolated skills.

The new focus in reading was very different. In the new reading definition, the state highlighted for the first time that readers bring something to their reading (their prior knowledge) that influences the meaning they construct of text. The definition also stated that readers have different purposes for reading (the context of reading), which shape readers' interpretations of text. These ideas suggested that each reader might construct a different meaning of text. This shift in focus implied radically different ways of thinking about reading instruction. First, reading comprehension rather than acquisition of skills became the main focus for reading. Second, student ideas, experiences, and purposes for reading became factors in understanding how readers read and interpret text. Teachers would have to learn how to help students make sense of text, rather than merely recognize words, and would need greater insight into who their students were and what they were thinking.

Policy documents accompanying the new definition also included the idea of readers' using strategies to read more effectively. These strategies were of two sorts. The first were cognitive strategies that good readers use to make sense of text, including such things as predicting events in a story, summarizing information, and monitoring comprehension. These strategies help readers think about their own thinking and regulate it as they are reading. The second kind of strategies involved understanding the organization of narrative text. These strategies help readers understand how stories unfold and how different parts of stories (setting, character, theme) are related.

The strategies are useful in helping readers recall story events and concepts more readily. Although good readers know and use these strategies intuitively, the policy suggested that they can also be taught to help "nonstrategic" readers read more effectively (MRA, 1987). As did ideas about prior knowledge and multiple interpretations, the idea of teaching reading strategies implied great changes in reading instruction. Teachers had to learn how to teach the strategies and how to help students use them effectively.

State policymakers knew their work implied big changes for many teachers. As one policymaker recalled, teachers reacted to the new definition with great anxiety, seeing it as "too extreme" and too difficult for them and their students to carry out. Another key policymaker said the policy required teachers to "reprogram their radar" so that they could see reading as a process of making sense of text rather than a process of collecting skills. A third characterized many teachers' responses to the policy as "overt hostility." Alongside the skeptical practitioners were a cadre of practitioners for whom the policy was familiar territory. The same policymaker who commented on teachers' overt hostility to the policy said that other teachers responded, "Finally, well, it's about time." For these practitioners, as for the policymakers themselves, the policy was the state's attempt to play catch-up. The ideas espoused in it, although new for state policies, were quite familiar to the reading research community, of which most of the key policymakers were members. Part of their motivation to change the state's perspective on reading was to help align reading instruction with the best, most up-to-date research on reading instruction. The policymakers' challenge was to marshal the support of the already converted to help others see the light. But how could they help teachers learn and believe?

As their comments illustrate, policymakers knew that their efforts implied that teachers had to learn new ideas about reading in order to change their practices. Yet it was not so clear *what* and *how* policymakers thought teachers might need to learn. This was to be expected. The ideas about reading were new. No other state had yet attempted to define reading in this way and certainly no state had undertaken an effort to help teachers learn how to carry out these new ideas in practice. Michigan policymakers were faced with a massive pedagogical task for which they had no models to follow and few colleagues to consult.

To carry out the policy's ideas in practice, teachers would have to learn about the ideas, but they would also have to learn from them. Whereas the first kind of "learning" is largely a matter of raising teachers' awareness of the policy by giving them information about it, the latter implies, to traditional teachers at least, acquiring new ways of thinking about reading. The two kinds of learning are not necessarily distinct from one another. Sproull (1981) makes an argument, in fact, that how practitioners are made aware of policies shapes how they implement them. Nor are they unusual. Cohen and Barnes (1993) suggest that by definition new policies contain new ideas or new configurations of old ideas (there would be little reason for them otherwise) and therefore imply some acquisition of new ways of thinking.

These two kinds of learning raise different pedagogical problems for policymakers. Making practitioners aware of a policy is essentially a problem of giving information (what Jackson [1986] might label reproductive learning). The way in which information is given may shape what practitioners do with it, but some learning is necessary for teachers to be aware of a policy. Helping practitioners make sense of new ideas and acquire new understandings is a matter not of having practitioners reproduce knowledge about policy given to them, but of transforming knowledge into ideas that make sense to them.

Thus, for the reading policy, teacher learning was a complex issue. Teachers had to be made aware of the changes in the policy and learn new conceptions of reading and new ideas about reading from the policy. What did policymakers do to help teachers learn? Did their actions appear to take into account both kinds of learning?

THE PERSPECTIVE OF THE STATE
DEPARTMENT OF EDUCATION

How did the policy makers try to train the practioners in the new policy?

Policymakers concentrated their work in four areas: They wrote the new definition of reading; developed new goals and objectives; organized several state-sponsored reading conferences to introduce their ideas to teachers; and, finally, developed a new state assessment for reading (the MEAP test). These four efforts and the documents surrounding them made up the state policy for reading. It was codified when the State Board of Education adopted the new definition in 1985 and when the revised MEAP test in reading was administered statewide for the first time in the fall of 1989.

The cornerstone of the state's effort to teach teachers about the new ideas about reading was a series of reading conferences held around the state. These conferences were two- or three-day events in which participants were introduced to the ideas of the policy in large-group orientation meetings, and then in small-group sessions were taught practical applications of the policy such as new classroom activities and reading strategies. These small-group sessions were called "modules" and were designed to demonstrate one reading strategy and/or activity that could be used in the classroom. The conferences generated a great deal of interest among practitioners and attendance at these conferences was significantly larger than policymakers expected. One policymaker estimated that 1,300 people attended one conference alone. All were surprised by the large numbers at all three of the major conferences. As one state reformer said: "I can't even begin to add up the number of people it [the definition] has been presented to. I mean it's just pretty overwhelming."

Despite the large numbers of participants at the state conferences, reformers' effort reached only a small percentage of teachers. Other teachers in the state needed to learn about the policy as well. To spread policy awareness beyond those who attended the conferences, policymakers provided participants with scripts of each of the conference sessions, so that participants could deliver the same lessons about the policy to teachers in their own districts. One policymaker said the purpose of scripting the modules and giving them to those who attended the conferences was that attendees could then "go do what we [reformers] did" to teachers in their districts. These conferences, in fact, were dubbed "The Training of Trainers" conferences because the goal from the very beginning was to train people to spread the word of the policy to others.

Conference participants did spread the word. Many districts throughout the state used conference scripts and other materials to stage workshops about the new definition of reading for their own teachers. For example, Mr. Fielder attended a weeklong reading in-service program on the policy in his district. The organizers used scripts and materials from the state conferences to tell teachers in their district about the new ideas in the state initiative. During much of this program, in fact, teachers in Mr. Fielder's district heard the same words teachers who had attended the state conferences heard.

Along with the state conferences and their local replications, policymakers saw the new MEAP test as a vehicle for teacher learning. Some talked about the test "driving" instruction in that it would make teachers aware of new questions to ask students and new ideas about text. Other policymakers talked about the test as being the only real leverage they had to make practitioners listen to their ideas. Policymakers saw the MEAP as a vehicle for learning in that it was an incentive (or perhaps a "stick," depending on one's perspective) for teachers to think about the policy. MEAP scores are very important in Michigan. They are publicly reported and are often used by people as measures of the worth of school districts. Until these changes in the MEAP, many schools, particularly those in middle-class districts, scored quite high on the tests. After the revisions, scores plummeted. The new tests sent many district administrators scrambling to figure out how to change instruction so that students in their districts would regain high scores.

Changes in the MEAP were significant. On the test, students read longer passages of "authentic" text (rather than segments contrived solely for the test) to assess comprehension. They were given expository as well as narrative text to read, and they were asked about their interest in and familiarity with topics about which they read. Although the main purpose for revising the test was to assess more appropriately students' reading abilities, some policymakers thought the test also might encourage teachers to use new instructional practices. For example, policymakers' purpose for including longer passages (in some cases complete stories) was to assess students' comprehension more completely, especially students' ability to comprehend the overall theme or idea of a piece of text. But policymakers also thought that if the revised test included longer passages of text, teachers might begin to have their students read longer pieces of text in class to better prepare them to take the MEAP. As one writer of the test said:

> Of course I don't want the effect of the test to stop there. But, the point is if some teacher who is now only using workbooks with 50 word paragraphs . . . decides that her kids need more practice reading full-length material so that they can take the MEAP, then you've had a tremendous impact even if the teacher doesn't understand exactly what is important about the material.

As a vehicle for teacher learning about the policy, then, the MEAP was seen by policymakers in two ways. The first was as a representation of their new ideas, which teachers could read, reflect on, come to understand, and therein learn from. The second was as a motivator to encourage new teacher behaviors in classrooms. Whether teachers "learned" from the new behaviors or from the ideas from which they stemmed was of secondary importance.

State policymakers faced a daunting task in teaching teachers about the policy. They had many teachers across the state to teach and to most of these teachers, the ideas policymakers were teaching were quite foreign. In addition, policymakers had few, if any, models of teaching teachers these new ideas. So, like many teachers faced with large and uncertain teaching tasks, policymakers taught the way they knew how. The conference sessions were conducted using very traditional pedagogy. Participants sat in chairs and listened to presenters tell them new ideas. Spin-off workshops and conferences in districts often followed the same format. Teachers had few, if any, opportunities to learn new ideas about reading or reading instruction in new pedagogical ways or to reconstruct what they were learning. Many of the learning opportunities centered on new activities or behaviors for teachers to adopt rather than opportunities for teachers to construct their own meaning of the policy and to develop their own new classroom actions. Teachers were to learn the "correct" lessons on how to teach reading in new ways. If they didn't, teachers ran the risk of low MEAP test scores.

That policymakers would employ traditional pedagogy to teach teachers about their efforts may not be unusual, but it is in this case ironic. The policy itself is based on the idea that learners construct meaning of new information in different ways because of their different prior experiences, yet policymakers acted as if all teachers, once made aware of the policy, would make the same sense of it and would implement the new ideas and activities, intact, in their classrooms.

Looking at the kinds of opportunities policymakers constructed for teachers, it is unclear whether policymakers understood that *how* teachers learned about the policy might be important and therefore should be different from traditional staff-development efforts. Listening to their talk, it is also unclear *what* exactly they wanted teachers to learn. Policymakers would say different things about it and all seemed to construct different images of appropriate practice as they went along. Some policymakers saw the policy as advocating "whole language"—children socially constructing meaning of text in their classrooms, whereas others viewed it as based in cognitive psychology with individual readers' constructing their own meaning. One reading teacher who attended the state conferences, helped develop other staff-development programs, and was familiar with the MEAP said she had a hard time putting together the big picture of the policy. She said she could derive no clear images of practice from her learning. For instance, how did the idea of longer text passages, which practitioners saw in the MEAP, fit with teaching metacognitive strategies that they were exposed to in the in-service training? How did any of these ideas make reading a dynamic, interactive process? What were teachers supposed to do with more than one "right" interpretation of text? What should reading practice look like if it followed the policy's vision?

Policymakers' efforts to help teachers learn about and from the policy presented a mixed picture. They took greater than usual care to construct opportunities for teachers to learn about the policy over a longer than usual period of time in that they organized many conferences for a number of years and held them throughout the state. They also provided districts with help in designing their own conferences on the reading policy so that more teachers could learn about the new ideas. Policymakers then did not rely on conferences alone, but revised state assessment as another learning tool connected to the policy. But even though their efforts were more extensive and enduring, they were limited in nature. Could teachers learn the new ideas about reading from the kind of opportunities they were given? What would they learn, if they did?

TEACHERS LEARNING FROM POLICY

Researchers also do not put teachers' learning from policy in clear perspective. Rather, they consider it from different perspectives, addressing the central questions of how teachers might learn from policies and what they might need to learn in order to implement them. For instance, much of the policy implementation literature focuses on external factors in teachers' environments that shape their responses to policy. These include such things as the structure of schooling (Meyer & Rowan, 1978; Weick, 1976); the relationship between policymakers and practitioners (Firestone, 1989; McLaughlin, 1990); the nature of policymaker's and practitioner's work (Lipsky, 1980); and the conditions and circumstances in which practitioners operate (Johnson & O'Connor, 1979; Lieberman, 1982; Schwille et al., 1983).

This literature is helpful in that it suggests that policies and practice are not tightly linked and that "policy as implemented often seems different from policy adopted" (Baier, March, & Saetren, 1988, p. 150). In this view, Mr. Fielder made changes in his reading practice because of the new reading policy, but those changes may be quite distinct from those of another teacher, because circumstances and resources in their work are different. This literature does not help us gain a clearer view of the role teacher learning plays in implementation of policy ideas. Even the few studies that mention learning as a factor in implementing policy reforms do not often consider how and what the learning might look like. Nor do they consider the relationship between what and how teachers learn and how they enact policy in their classrooms. Elmore and McLaughlin (1988) state that to carry out new educational reforms teachers must acquire conceptual understandings of the reform and will need more than traditional staff-development opportunities to do so. McDonnell and Elmore (1987) also suggest that practitioners may need to learn to build their capacities to carry out policies. These studies are notable in that they are among the few that consider learning as a factor in teachers' making sense of policies, but they too touch only lightly on the actual learning process.

The *learning process* that teachers go through is still a mystery. There are elements, though, that point toward understanding by examining the learning process and by looking at individuals' responses to policy. The implementation literature looks at teachers as members of a group, that is, as people whose work has a similar nature or who experience the same working conditions. The implicit assumption of the standard policy implementation study is that similarities in environment will result in similarities in response to policies. Considering group characteristics may not be a particularly useful lens through which to look at teachers' learning from policy. Many ideas about learning come from cognitive psychology and focus on the role a learner's personal orientations play in learning. This body of research conveys the image of learners' taking in new information by assimilating it with what they already know and how they already perceive the world (Anderson, 1984; Anderson, Reynolds, Schallert, & Goetz, 1977; Rumelhart, 1980). Who learners are (what experiences, ideas, and beliefs they have) will shape how they make sense of new information they receive, and in the process of assimilation both old and new ideas may change to "fit" together. Learning is a process of harmonizing new and old ideas. New ideas are interpreted in unique ways by learners because of what they already know and believe. This suggests that the issue of teachers' learning from policy may have to be looked at with a finer grain. How teachers learn from policy and how they play it out in their classrooms may have less to do with external factors in their environment than with characteristics of individual learners.

A few policy researchers have looked at the policy/practice relationship as one that individual practitioners construct. These studies consider how individual practitioners' perceptions of policies shape the ways in which policies play out (Cohen, March, & Olsen, 1972; *Educational Evaluation and Policy Analysis* [*EEPA*], 1990; Keisler & Sproull, 1982; Kingdon, 1984; McLaughlin, 1987; Weiss & Cohen, 1991). They suggest that how policies are attended to and how they are perceived is shaped by practitioners' existing beliefs and capacities. McLaughlin (1987) writes:

Change is ultimately the problem of the smallest unit. At each point in the policy process, a policy is transformed as individuals interpret and respond to it. What actually is delivered or provided under the aegis of a policy depends finally on the individual at the end of the line. (p. 174)

This literature is helpful in that it suggests that the individual's interpretation of policy actually influences practice. Policy therefore is largely what practitioners perceive it to be rather than some external document or legislation. In this view, Mr. Fielder may change his reading practice in a way that is quite distinct from other teachers not solely because his environment differs, but because he interprets the policy to mean different things.

The "policy-as-perceived" literature helps us understand individual responses to policy and introduces the notion that what is implemented is not just a reflection of what is adopted, because implementation is mediated through the individual practitioner's beliefs and experiences. This research, though, stops at the point of suggesting that practitioners uniquely perceive policies. It says little about how practitioners come to perceive policies. What beliefs, capacities, experiences, influence practitioners' perceptions? If practitioners' perceptions shape policies, what shapes practitioners' perceptions? Where, if at all, does learning fit?

The final body of literature that bears on the issue of teachers' learning from policy is that which looks at teacher education itself, but there are very few studies that consider the learning process of teachers (Carter, 1990). There is research that suggests fruitful lines of inquiry. Some studies, particularly those that consider educating teachers to teach in new ways, focus on what teachers need to know, especially how much and what kind of subject-matter knowledge might be necessary for teachers (Shulman, 1987; Wilson, Shulman, & Richert, 1987). In these studies, learning and knowledge are important components in helping teachers learn to teach, but the nature of the learning process is underdeveloped.

Other studies look at how novice teachers acquire the knowledge they use to teach. Hollingsworth's (1989) study of 14 preservice teachers learning to teach reading suggests the influence of existing beliefs on learning. In this study, preservice teachers' beliefs about teaching, learning, and reading "served as filters" for processing ideas they encountered both in their coursework and in their field experiences. Kagan (1992), in a review of teacher education literature, summarized 27 studies on beginning teachers' learning that support the idea that what preservice and beginning teachers learn is shaped by the ideas, beliefs, and experiences with teaching and learning that they bring to their professional education.

Among experienced teachers, the importance of personal ideas, beliefs, and experiences is suggested in a series of research articles on teachers' personal, practical knowledge (Clandinin, 1985; Johnson, 1989). Experienced teachers understand teaching through a special knowledge that
they develop from theories about learning and teaching and from their
practical experiences. This knowledge is "blended by the personal back-
ground and characteristics of the teacher and expressed by her in particular situations" (Clandinin, 1985, p. 362.) Learning to teach in these studies
has much to do with the personal nature of teacher/learners—who they
are and what they bring to their learning—as well as the context in which
they work.

These studies of both preservice and experienced teachers fit well
with the cognitive psychology perspective. What teachers bring to their
learning shapes how they process new information. This suggests that
what teachers bring to their encounters with policies influences how they
perceive policies, and the learning they may do in connection with the
policy as well. But policies, in general, do not become policies merely to
affect the learning of practitioners. Their purpose is to change things that
practitioners do. So how, if at all, does this view of learning affect what
teachers "do" with policies? What is the relationship among teachers'
learning from policy, their perceptions of it, and changes in their classrooms?

One theory grounded in cognitive psychology suggests that change
in beliefs and ideas occurs when new ideas can no longer be assimilated
to existing frameworks because discrepancies—that is, dissonance or dis-
harmonies—between new and old ideas become too numerous or too
great. When this happens, new ideas help create new frameworks that
become the frameworks with which succeeding information is processed
(Bruner, 1983; Posner, Strike, Hewson, & Gertzog, 1983). Kennedy (1991)
applies this idea of dissonance and learning directly to change in teaching
practices. She suggests that for teachers to learn new ideas, they must first
be made aware of differences between their existing practices and the
new ideas. One way in which teachers can be made aware is through vivid
images of new practices. For change to occur, new ideas about teaching
must be startling enough to provoke a sense of dissonance so that teachers
cannot easily assimilate the new ideas into their existing practices. Hollingsworth (1989) noted that preservice teachers changed their beliefs
about teaching and learning when they faced some dissonance between
their own beliefs and those of their cooperating teachers. In working out
the dissonance, these preservice teachers gained richer understandings
about teaching reading than did those preservice teachers who did not
encounter any challenges. This view of learning suggests that for teachers

to undertake change because of a policy change, they must perceive dissonance between their current practices and the policy's ideas. They then have to be willing to learn new ideas and to enact them to reduce the dissonance that they themselves have created. This suggestion puts us into a bewildering loop—if policies are only what teachers perceive them to be, what would be necessary for them to perceive dissonance? Change and learning are difficult tasks for most people. What would a policy have to do to start the process of perceiving dissonance, learning, and then change?

Thus there is no single map to guide the analysis of how and what teachers learn from policy and what changes in practice play out. The state's efforts to help teachers learn are a mélange of new ideas taught with old pedagogies and pieces of changed reading practices, not a coherent picture. State policymakers wanted teachers to teach reading in new ways, and they thought that opportunities to learn about the policy might do the trick. Research literature on teacher learning and the relationship between policy and practice points to problems about the efficacy of the state effort, but leaves many unanswered questions about the relationships among learning, interpretation, and implementation. How do teachers interpret learning opportunities related to a policy? What and how did teachers make sense of learning opportunities surrounding policy? What did teachers perceive themselves as needing to learn? And how do teachers' interpretation of policies and the learning they asked to do affect changes they make in practice?

These are the questions this book explores. Specifically, it looks at the relationships among teachers' perceptions of the Michigan reading policy, their learning in connection with it, and how they change their reading practices. These relationships are interconnected and complex. To explore them requires looking carefully at individuals and listening to what they say about their learning, their understanding of policy, and their reading practices. It also requires looking at what individuals do in their classrooms and then attempting to link in some way what they say about their learning and understanding of the reading policy and how they teach reading.

CHAPTER 2

Catherine Price: Doing the Policy

Kingdon (1984) writes that public policy is not the brainchild of any single actor, but rather is the outgrowth of ideas that already exist in a community. The ideas precede the actual formation of a policy, and therefore, most often, someone is "doing" the policy long before it is enacted.

Catherine Price is a teacher who has been doing the reading policy for some time. Since the 1950s, when she began teaching, Ms. Price has believed that comprehension of text should be the focus of reading instruction and that children's prior knowledge and experiences shape the sense they make of text. She has had a literature-based reading program for many years and has included expository text in her instruction as well. So ideas such as the emphasis on comprehension, expository text, and readers' prior knowledge that are associated with the policy are not new to Ms. Price.

Even so, Ms. Price speaks of learning new things from the policy. She says she learned about writing from a workshop on the policy that she attended. She says she learned a new language. Finally, she says she learned from and about the policy through other ideas she could connect to it. Each of these experiences shaped Ms. Price's thinking about the policy and, ultimately, shaped the effect the policy had on her teaching practice.

Ms. Price's past beliefs and practices, and her new learning from the policy, set her apart as a teacher attempting ambitious instructional practices. Ms. Price describes herself as an innovator who continually tries new ideas to find better ways to teach her students. Her ambitious practices are not always easy to pull off. Ms. Price speaks of tensions she experiences in her teaching between her desire to have a child-centered classroom in which student interest and choice set the curriculum and her belief that children need to learn certain ideas and information in school.

In Ms. Price's case, this tension is most apparent in her literacy instruction. She places a high value on students' directing their own learning to read and write and provides students many opportunities to decide what and when they read and write. At the same time, she thinks students need to develop a repertoire of reading and language skills and abilities that she can best help them acquire through direct, planned instruction. Ms. Price can often work toward both of these goals with little conflict, but sometimes these goals demand different kinds of instruction and responses to student thinking. At these times, Ms. Price struggles over which way to go. The new ideas she associates with the policy seem to her to suggest even greater student control over their learning, and therefore the policy contributes to the tensions that Ms. Price already experiences.

How has Ms. Price's learning from the policy played out in her practices? Does her new learning contribute the tensions she already faces?

BACKGROUND

Ms. Price has taught for over 30 years. She began teaching at age 18 when she entered a teaching order of nuns immediately after high school. While teaching, she graduated from college and received a master's degree in education. A few years ago, Ms. Price left the convent and taught in a private alternative school run by friends. Although she loved teaching in this school, which she thought was in harmony with her beliefs about how children learn, she felt that her own professional growth called her to teach in public schools. For the last five years, she has been teaching a fifth/sixth-grade classroom of underachieving gifted students at Lewis School.

Students in Ms. Price's class have been identified from a variety of tests as highly able but working below their abilities. The purpose of the program in which Ms. Price teaches is to help these students work up to their learning potential. She commented that many of her students are referred to her program because they are troublemakers in "normal" classrooms, although she sees little difference between the students she now has in her class and those she has always taught. She claims that her teaching hasn't changed because she is teaching a class of "gifted" students. She would do what she does—and has done what she does—for all kinds of students. She said, "I don't see myself as being in an irregular classroom. I think I've always taught this way. If I were in a regular classroom I'd do the same things I'm doing."

All the attention to gifted education is a bit surprising in this district. Drummond is a district with little money for extra programs and limited administrative staff to direct them. The gifted program is funded in a joint effort with the neighboring school district. Children from both districts can attend either the underachieving program in which Ms. Price teaches or more traditional gifted classes whose focus is to move students through the curriculum at an accelerated pace.

Drummond school district is comprised of three small towns—Drummond, Lewis, and Blakely. The superintendent of schools, John O'Malley, describes the community as predominantly blue-collar with most of the population working as skilled laborers in a nearby auto plant or railroad yard. Few residents hold supervisory or executive positions. Many trace their roots to Eastern Europe. The population is stable, little in- or out-migration, and there are few minorities. The superintendent said that most residents support the schools but generally have low academic expectations for their children.

Lewis, the town in the district in which Ms. Price teaches, consists of houses, a video store, a few bars, a grain elevator, and a vinyl siding company. Even on sunny days, the town looks tired. The school is one of the better kept buildings in town. It is one of four elementary schools in the district. It draws students from families in the middle range of economic status in the district. Likewise, Lewis's students consistently score in the middle range for the district on standardized tests. According to the principal, most of the staff at Lewis has taught together for many years. Although there is a friendly atmosphere in the school among the staff, there is a clear division between teachers who see themselves as progressive educators and those who do not. Ms. Price falls into the former group.

DISTRICT EFFORTS ASSOCIATED WITH
THE READING POLICY

Both Superintendent O'Malley and Lewis's principal, Ned Abbott, described the district's attention to the reading policy as significant. O'Malley said that changes asked for in the reading definition were "the biggest and most difficult" ones the district had undertaken, but some of the most important. Personally, he said he likes the reading policy's focus because he sees it helping students learn to "enjoy reading" and to "see reading as more than just a class." O'Malley's goal for reading instruction in the district is that "every kid will read." Abbott echoed many of O'Malley's comments. He too saw the policy as representing big changes for many staff members, although he thought teachers in his school would generally be more receptive to the changes than teachers in the other elementary schools in the district. Abbott characterized his staff as willing to consider new ideas and willing to work to improve the instruction they offer students.

O'Malley and Abbott credit the district's two reading consultants with bringing the state's reading policy to the teachers. The reading consultants worked with state policymakers to design the state reading conferences and to revise the Michigan Educational Assessment Program (MEAP) reading test. When the reading consultants talked to O'Malley and Abbott about the state policy, they were encouraged to plan ways to help Drummond teachers learn the new ideas. The reading consultants approached this task in three ways. First, they planned a five-day workshop for teachers focused on the state policy. The workshop, called Reading Update, consisted of short sessions that highlighted different features of the policy. Sessions dealt with theories from cognitive psychology that introduced teachers to some of the research underlying the policy, new classroom activities for teachers to use in their reading practice, and use of new materials. Teachers selected sessions to attend and were instructed to share what they learned with others. This five-day workshop became so popular with teachers and administrators that the reading consultants offered it numerous times over a three-year period. Workshops were offered over an extended period of time with more and more teachers attending; conversations in the district about reading and the reading policy were kept current.

The second approach to helping teachers understand the new reading policy was to work with them in their classrooms and to continue discussions about new reading practices in staff meetings. After attending Reading Update, many teachers were excited about the ideas they heard, but uneasy about how to translate them into new reading practices. Much of the consultants' time over the three-year period in which they offered the reading workshops was spent working with individual teachers in classrooms, talking about the ideas at every available opportunity. Abbott allotted one teachers' meeting a month to the reading consultant to talk about reading. These discussions focused on new activities teachers could use or addressed problems some teachers encountered as they tried out the new ideas. In Ms. Price's school, these monthly teachers' meetings resulted in the formation of a teachers' study group that worked on how to use expository text with students. Other teachers began to request individual help from the reading consultants. Teresa Jensen, Lewis's reading consultant, said about her work in the time period after Reading Update:

> I've tried for years to get away from a pull-out program and tried to be more of a coach or mentor or whatever with teachers. And this year, it's really exciting because I've had more teachers say, "Would

you come in and show me or come in and watch me do it [a new
reading practice]?" And when they say, "Will you watch me do it?"
it's really wonderful. So it's been awhile, but I think it [the work-
shop] has really impacted people.

The third approach the reading consultants used was to establish
what they called "teacher networks" so that teachers within and outside
of the district could talk to each other about reading. The consultants saw
their workshops as places where teachers could begin to make connections with others who were interested in changing their reading practices
and they saw their mission after the workshops as facilitating teacher
groups. Jensen commented:

> We've tried very hard to make it possible for people to continue to
> talk with each other. We've put together some meetings after school
> where people can network. For instance, one presenter at Reading
> Update talked about reciprocal teaching. So we had her come back
> and talk again so that people could go away, try something out, and
> touch base with her and say, "Well, it worked" or "Well, it didn't
> work." . . . We encouraged people to network. We wanted to lay the
> foundation for collegial sharing. That's the biggest factor—teachers
> communicating with each other.

Many teacher groups formed to discuss reading instruction and Ms.
Jensen saw this as the most effective way of helping teachers learn and
change.

The final approach for the reading consultants was to purchase a new
literature-based basal series for the district and to provide money for
teachers who wished to use trade books in their classrooms to teach reading. This approach was not without its difficulties. Many teachers saw the
state policy as pushing them away from using any sort of basal textbook
series. These teachers advocated using textbook funds to buy literature
for classrooms. Other teachers, those perhaps less enamored of the policy's ideas, pushed hard for the purchase of some kind of basal reader.
They believed that many teachers needed a new kind of textbook to help
them make the changes they saw the policy asking them to make. This
split in ideas resulted in what O'Malley called a "fractured committee" and
the textbook adoption process, which normally takes one year, took three.
In the end, a "literature-based" basal series was purchased. Although the
divisiveness on the committee was difficult, it did keep changes in reading
instruction in the forefront and, as one of the reading consultant com-

mented, engaged even those teachers reluctant to change in conversations about reading.

District efforts to bring the new ideas of the state reading policy into Ms. Price's district, then, were extensive and enduring, two qualities that are often not characteristic of a district's response to changes in state policy. Teachers had multiple opportunities to learn about the new policy and new ways of thinking about reading instruction. They also had these opportunities over an extended period of time. What sense did Ms. Price make of them?

MS. PRICE'S EXISTING BELIEFS AND PRACTICES

Beliefs About Teaching and Learning

Ms. Price is an eager learner who for her entire adult life has been engaged with ideas about teaching and learning. She attends many conferences and classes on new instructional approaches. She reads voraciously, both professional books and fiction. She has been involved with numerous district and county committees in charge of redesigning curriculum. At times, Ms. Price almost seems to take in ideas indiscriminately. In talking about her views of teaching and learning, she mentions John Dewey and a new book on brain patterns put out by the Association for Supervision and Curriculum Development in the same sentence, and each seems to have the same degree of influence on her beliefs about experiential learning. So Ms. Price's beliefs stem from both well-established educational philosophy and more current educational ideas that strike her fancy for shorter periods of time.

Ms. Price describes her teaching as child-centered. She thinks the crucial factor in any learning experience is what students are interested in and what their abilities are. Her role is to keep a sense of a curriculum that she wants to teach, but to mediate that curriculum with her understanding of what and where her students are intellectually. When I asked her if there was a district curriculum that she followed, she said that there was, but that it was not the only piece she considered when constructing her practices:

> I have my basic curriculum and we go with it . . . but is there a curriculum beyond it? Definitely. The child—where the child takes the curriculum. So that the curriculum is what it is, but basically students are going to help direct that curriculum by who they are.

To find out who they are, Ms. Price talks about "dancing" with her students. She discovered this metaphor in a book she recently read called *The Dancing Wu Li Masters* (Zukav, 1980) in which a martial arts instructor talks about finding his students' "centers" and dancing with them until they are interested in dancing alone. The dancing that Ms. Price sees as necessary involves uncovering her students' abilities and interests and mixing them with her sense of a curriculum—topics, objectives, subject-matter knowledge, and resources. The goal of the dance is for students to be their own teachers—to follow their own interests without a master. But Ms. Price sees the dance as tricky because it means finding students' centers and convincing them to incorporate new ideas into their dance.

In her classroom, Ms. Price's beliefs in child-centered instruction manifest themselves in a great deal of student choice and individualized instruction. During large portions of the day, students are free to work on their own projects. They can choose where they wish to work and with whom they wish to collaborate, as well as what work they do at any given time. Ms. Price spends hours after school writing up individual instructional plans for students so that everyone is working at an appropriate level and on topics that hold some interest to them. A great deal of time is devoted to reading during the day. On some days I saw as much as an hour of silent reading time in which students read a variety of materials, from wrestling magazines to Charles Dickens.

Another important belief Ms. Price holds is that people learn best when they can connect ideas and experiences. Connections must occur between what they already know and new ideas. Connections also must occur among the new ideas and information students are learning. Ms. Price says she sees learners not taking in new ideas *unless they can see connections.* She said, "If I don't see connections, I will not take things in. I won't have anything to do with them. I use the term connections a lot because I see in it very much a basis for learning."

One way Ms. Price helps students see connections is by integrating her instruction—a practice many teachers, principals, and state policymakers came to associate with the reading policy. When I first asked her if I could observe her teach reading, she replied that I would have to watch her all day. Although she puts a schedule on the board each morning that delineates a time for each subject, she says she is teaching all of them all the time. The schedule is only to keep students who need order happy. Ms. Price chooses books to read in language arts that deal with topics studied in social studies or science. She has students write during mathematics so that they can see how an algebraic expression relates to a sentence with various components that make up a complete idea. She thinks of overarching themes for her instruction such as balance or interdependence and then works the themes into her instruction across the day and year. When I asked her if she teaches the various subjects differently, she said she didn't think so because she was "trying very hard to integrate" and she really thought "it is happening."

The other way Ms. Price helps students connect is through "hands-on" activities. She sees these as useful in connecting what happens in school with out-of-school interests. Students were engaged in at least one activity-based lesson on each day that I observed. One day they worked on a social studies simulation in which they acted as pioneers moving west in covered wagons. Another day, they "discovered" properties of weights and balances by designing race cars and running them on home-made tracks. Ms. Price talked about these activities as "hooks to reel students in" by making what they learn in school have relevance to the outside world. In the social studies simulation, for instance, one of her goals was for students to connect what they experienced—making decisions as part of a wagon train—with what pioneers might actually have experienced and thereby become aware of how difficult and frightening pioneers' lives were.

Many of Ms. Price's beliefs about teaching and learning foreshadowed some of the ideas of the reading policy—making reading an integral part of each subject studied throughout the day, connecting what children experience and already know with what they learn in school, asserting the importance of children's prior knowledge and understanding in the learning process. But observing Ms. Price teach also revealed some beliefs about which the policy is silent. There are skills that Ms. Price thinks are essential for students to learn regardless of their individual interests or prior experiences. These include grammar, punctuation, and use of literary devices. For instance, Ms. Price wanted her students to be able to identify cause-and-effect relationships between events in text. To give them practice in doing so, Ms. Price gave them a worksheet designed to instruct students on this skill by requiring them to read short passages of text and answering cause and effect questions on them. This lesson was a separate skill lesson taught to the whole class and not integrated with the text they were reading together.

Ms. Price also demands careful reading of text and has taught students how to use text to support interpretations. In many of the discussions about novels the class was reading, Ms. Price would pointedly question students about events in the story when they were offering interpretations of text. During a discussion of *The Call of the Wild*, for example, a student was making a claim that Buck was becoming a leader. Ms. Price questioned him, "What did Buck do to show leadership?" At first the student did not respond, but then he looked at the text and answered, "He stole other dogs' food." Only after he found this support in the text for his claim did Ms. Price let him continue. Interwoven with an open, child-centered pedagogy that would look very pleasing to many state reformers was some teacher-controlled, didactic pedagogy aimed at transmitting a fixed set of ideas and practices to students.

Given the policy's silence on how a teacher might teach skills or the warrant for textual interpretation, it is difficult to know if reformers would agree with Ms. Price's decisions. Would they support separate skill lessons or careful reading of text? Would they suggest other practices? Reformers' lack of guidance in how teachers might embed skill instruction in meaningful literacy events raises questions about whether Ms. Price is "doing" the policy. For some reformers, she may not be. Or she may be doing much more—that is, constructing a more comprehensive literacy practice that deals with all aspects of literacy students traditionally have learned in school, even those on which the policy is silent. More examples from Ms. Price's reading and language arts practice will illustrate this.

Her Practice

> All the literature that's out will tell you to get a book started with something that will hook them right away. Sometimes you don't have to work very hard at it, sometimes you do and sometimes it is just painful. But I think if it doesn't happen then you shouldn't go on with it.

Teaching Literature. Ms. Price's main goal in reading a book in class is to provide something that students will find meaningful in their lives. An avid reader, Ms. Price sees reading as an important part of her own life and she often shares her enthusiasm about books with her students. She reads on a wide range of topics and will hunt up books on a subject that she knows interests one of her students. Ms. Price said she has found one of the truly successful things she does to motivate reluctant readers is to read a book with them and discuss it. This means she is frequently reading children's books on topics that may not be to her personal taste but that she knows make a difference to students. As she commented about her reading instruction:

> I dwell on the small ways to let them succeed in reading and I have to just watch to see what those are. I have to dance with them. I really do. I have to feel where they are.

Ms. Price's passion for and knowledge of literature are obvious in her instruction. As I learned in our first interview, she uses only trade books with her class, declining the district's offer of a literature-based reading text, which she sees as much less engaging for students. (Although Drummond bought new reading texts for all teachers, a number of teachers at Lewis said they used them sporadically if at all. This practice is—if not sanctioned—at least ignored by the principal, who supports teachers' judgment in using materials.) Students in Ms. Price's do a lot of individual reading. They can choose whatever they want to read during this time and Ms. Price has a wide range of books in her classroom for them. When she chooses texts for the whole class to read, she attempts to find titles that relate in some way to topics they are discussing in other subject areas, but primarily she is concerned with finding books that build on students' interests and prior experiences. In the two years I observed her, she read *The Call of the Wild* because she had a large group of boys in her class who were interested in hunting and outdoor life, and because it is a book she loves.

I watched Ms. Price teach *The Call of the Wild* on a few occasions. She introduced the book by asking students if they had read anything else by London. Many hands went up and various titles were shouted out. Some students said how "cool" they thought his stories were. One boy said he stayed up all night finishing *White Fang*. Ms. Price passed around a map of the Northwest Territories and the Yukon to show where most of the book takes place. She then delivered a knowledgeable and inspiring account of the author:

> If you remember, those of you who have read "To Build a Fire,"
> when Jack London wrote about needing to build a fire, you really
> felt like you needed a fire. Jack London wrote that story for a good
> reason. He was out making a living, trying to support his family in
> strange ways. He would deliver newspapers and do other odd jobs.
> He really struggled to provide food and a home. He liked adventure.
> He got into trouble because he took so many risks, but he never
> blamed others for his troubles. Some people compare trouble to a
> mountain. Some people walk around the mountain and they never
> have any trouble. Some people stop and turn away from it. Others
> go over it and have no trouble. But others willingly go through it,
> and feel it, feel what trouble is like, and come out stronger. That's
> what Jack London did.

She went on to tell students that even though some might have read the book before, they were going to read it very differently this time: "London does something in his writing to get the reader involved and I want you to think about that when you read. . . . We are going to look at the many levels of change that happen in the book. We're going to take a look at what it means to the dog, to the people in the story, and to ourselves." By this time, all students seemed very much engaged and listened attentively as Ms. Price read the first chapter.

Ms. Price said that she wanted to make sure her students could see the relevance of London's work to their lives. She commented:

> There's so much that is in this book that can be so profound for students, like the comparisons with humanity—human values and dog values. I need to help them find the comparisons. We'll do that in here. They'll build up to it.

Often in the lessons I observed, Ms. Price took care to point out what she considered beautiful or meaningful passages of text and to help students work through their meaning, as in this example: "'He felt oppressed by the vague sense of impending calamity.' That's a heavy sentence. . . . Have any of you been outside on a hot day working hard with no water? You feel pressed by the heat and the dryness. Well, the dog felt this. Pressed down by the sense that something terrible would happen." During another lesson, she asked, "What do you think the sentence, 'Far more potent were the memories of his heredity that made things he had never seen seem familiar' means?" Students responded to these questions of Ms. Price's with comments that reflected much more than literal comprehension of the words. For example, in response to her question about heredity, one student said that he thought the phrase referred to the dog's instinct, which meant he knew how to be wild like his ancestors and wanted to be wild in his heart. She often asked students to look for phrases or parts of the story they thought were beautiful, and to share them with the class.

Throughout her teaching of this novel, Ms. Price insisted that students stick very closely to the text when constructing their ideas about the book. Although students could respond to text in individual ways, Ms. Price kept pushing them to look at the text to support their claims. For students to recall details and events was important not as a way to check whether they had read the text but to help them understand what London was attempting to communicate in the book. The following is an example from a class discussion in which the relationships between the men and the dogs were the focus:

Ms. Price: What happened to Francois and Perrault? Look back in the paragraph.
Joe: They were dying?

Ms. Price: Did the book say that? Where does it say that?

Joe: I don't know.

Ms. Price: You can't just make things up. It has to be in the book.

Tony: I can say why Francois and Perrault put their arms around Buck.

Ms. Price: Okay, why?

Tony: Because they loved him.

Ms. Price: But where were they going?

Josh: It says they received official orders, so they must have been ordered to go elsewhere.

Ms. Price: Good. It's just one little sentence. It would be easy to miss. But, we don't want to miss things in the text.

This discussion continued for a time with Ms. Price asking students to go back to the text to recall what was really happening. She did so, it seemed, so that students would form interpretations that they could support with text. Students could not just make things up for Ms. Price. Even though her classroom is child-centered, it is not ruleless or without standards.

I found this "close-to-the-text" reading at first perplexing. The state reform says very little about text and offers no help for teachers in deciding how to use text in reading instruction. Most elementary classes I have seen either focus on students' emotional responses to text with little consideration of the text itself or focus on literal recall of text details and events with little consideration of the meaningfulness of the text. Ms. Price's instruction offers a synthesis. She stresses respect for the text and a need to use it to construct meaning, yet the importance of a close reading is to help students plumb the text to get the most out of it. Her goal in reading is to help students understand what authors are trying to communicate and, therein, find reading a meaningful experience.

Reading literature in Ms. Price's classroom centers on students' interests, thinking, and past experiences. This is very important to Ms. Price. She wants her students to see reading as being as vital to their lives as it is to hers. Yet her child-centered literature instruction does not mean that students can read and interpret text any way they wish. Ms. Price also teaches students the skill of using text to construct meaning and insists that their interpretations be warranted by examples from text. Another example of this was a discussion of *The Call of the Wild* in which Ms. Price asked students whether they thought Buck had changed after his kidnapping. Most students responded that he had because he had gotten stronger or more wild. Ms. Price asked them to read sentences in the book that supported their statements. One boy thought that Buck had remained the same and Ms. Price asked what in the text led him to that conclusion.

The boy said he couldn't find any *exact* sentences that made him feel that way, he just did. As the class shouted that he was wrong, Ms. Price said that everyone has a right to interpret stories they way they thought best, but that he needed some evidence to back up his thinking. She suggested he go back and reread the chapter to find what might have made him think that Buck had not changed and then report back to the class later.

For Ms. Price, there are rules for interpreting text to which she expects her students to adhere. "Feelings" are not in themselves enough of a warrant to justify constructing meaning of text. So Ms. Price's literature instruction covers two goals: first, to get students interested in reading by using their thinking and interests as starting points for instruction; and second, to help them learn how to read text and construct valid interpretations.

Whether Ms. Price's teaching of literature fits with visions in the policy is difficult to know. The issues of what literature to teach and how to teach it are not mentioned in the policy. Furthermore, although debates in literary criticism over textual interpretation are quite heated, the reading policy says nothing of them. Readers interpret text, according to the policy, but how they should do so is not specified. So a reformer might point out Ms. Price as a teacher "doing" the policy in that her practice has many signposts of the policy—that is, use of trade books, meaningful reading experiences—but in fact Ms. Price may have gone far beyond it. She addresses issues, such as interpretation of text, that the policy fails to address yet that teachers would have to consider if they took the policy seriously.

Language Arts Skills. In addition to reading literature, Ms. Price also teaches language arts skills—such things as punctuation, capitalization, literacy devices like cause and effect, and vocabulary. Although Ms. Price occasionally teaches skills through text the class is reading, most often she teaches separate lessons using worksheets she has gathered from different language arts instructional activity books. Ms. Price said that she teaches language arts skills to the whole class in separate lessons because she thinks all children need to know these things to read and write well and this is an efficient way of teaching them.

In a lesson I observed on punctuation and capitalization, students proofread a piece of text that had deliberately been written with many errors. Ms. Price introduced this work by asking students if they could share some strategies they used to know when to capitalize words:

RICKY: Whenever I see a dot, I know to capitalize the first letter in the next word.

Ms. Price: Ah . . . so when you see a period, you know the next
    letter is a capital. Another?
Katie: When you write I or the name of someone important.
Ms. Price: Does it have to be an important person?
Katie: No, just anyone's name.

The class went through a few more strategies together and then worked
on their papers individually. Ms. Price walked around helping students.
After about 20 minutes, students were directed to hand in the worksheet
and go on to the next subject.

A lesson on using cause and effect in text had a similar format. Ms.
Price passed out a worksheet labeled "Cause and Effect: Using cause and
effect to explain a historical event." It consisted of two passages, one
about the Wright Brothers and one on the *Mayflower*, and questions on
causes and effects explicated in the text—for example, for the Wright
Brothers, "What caused the glider to nose-dive into a sand dune?" Ms.
Price wrote the words *cause* and *effect* on the board and then had students read the passage about the *Mayflower*. She asked students to pick
out three examples of cause and effect in the passage.

Ms. Price: This is a hard one. Anyone have any?
Steven: However . . .
Ms. Price: [interrupting him] No. A cause-and-effect sentence would
    not likely start with however. Do you know what I mean by
    cause and effect? [Steven nods yes.] Anyone?
Tony: [reading from the passage] "He didn't like lubbers much."
Ms. Price: Is there someone who could help Tony?
Josh: They didn't get along.
Ms. Price: Okay. Where does it say that, Nick?
Nick: [reading] "There was friction."
Ms. Price: Okay. Nick, read the sentence that talks about there being
    friction.
Nick: "The average seaman of 1620 was an illiterate brawler who dis-
    liked 'lubbers.'"
Ms. Price: Good. So the cause is that seaman dislike lubbers and the
    effect is that there is friction.

The class worked through all examples and questions on the worksheet
in similar fashion: students reading a sentence that they thought showed
cause and effect, Ms. Price confirming or disconfirming their ideas with
little explanatory discourse, and, finally, Ms. Price's rephrasing or summarizing student ideas into coherent, "correct" answers.

Ms. Price teaches language skills separately from books students are reading as well as from their writing. This contrasts with other teachers' practices in which skills are almost always taught in context—through questions students have in their efforts to make sense of text—and certainly would not jive with some interpretations of the policy that suggest that skills not be taught as end goals in themselves. Ms. Price said she teaches skills this way because she thinks of them as tools all students need. And often students need to learn tools in contrived settings. She gave an example from a science project lesson:

> For instance, the other day I wanted them to summarize what it was that they had done in the "Our World in Motion" program. What we did was go over how to do a summary and then we learned how to do a summary, but we did it with other material that we understood. And so once we did that, then I gave them the task of summarizing the program.

Students needed to learn how to summarize text to help them learn. This was a skill and, in the above example at least, it appeared more beneficial to Ms. Price that they learn the skill in a decontextualized way *outside* of the text students ultimately had to summarize. In Ms. Price's view, language arts skills comprise knowledge that must be transmitted to students in order for them to be able to comprehend text at all. Teaching skills to the whole class using teacher-directed pedagogy, out of the context of their reading and writing, thus makes the most sense.

There are then two components that make up Ms. Price's reading/language arts practices: teaching literature and teaching language arts skills. These are sometimes related—for example, Ms. Price will teach a vocabulary lesson using words from the book the class is reading—but at other times are separate. And within both of these pieces, Ms. Price uses different pedagogies. Some lessons appear open-ended, going in the direction student interest takes them, and others appear very didactic—lessons in which Ms. Price is transmitting knowledge to students for them to take in.

Some of Ms. Price's beliefs and practices fit well with reformers' visions of the policy. One policymaker said that she thought model classrooms would be ones in which "instruction is driven by children." This fits with Ms. Price's idea of child-centered instruction. Another policymaker commented that he hoped teachers would be encouraged by the policy to use more literature to teach reading and would integrate reading with social studies and science. This, too, fits well with Ms. Price's use of literature and integrated instruction. A third policymaker talked about the importance of having students read long passages of text instead of short, basal entries. This connects with Ms. Price's using "real" literature rather than the basal textbook her district supplied. But it is difficult to know if policymakers would support other beliefs and practices employed by Ms. Price, particularly her approach to skills instruction. There is little advice in policy documents on how teachers should teach such topics as literary devices or punctuation and vocabulary. So in many ways Ms. Price's classroom might look like a model for reformers, but it is unclear whether all of her practices would look exemplary.

Ms. Price herself saw the policy as congruent with what she believes and does. Like many teachers, she said her first reaction to the policy was that she already did it. She said much of what she learned about the policy legitimated her existing ideas and was not new. And even though she saw her teaching as basically consistent with the policy's vision, she commented that she learned new things from it.

MS. PRICE'S LEARNING ABOUT AND FROM THE POLICY

Ms. Price's primary introduction to the reading policy was Reading Update, the week-long district in-service training program. Because many of the materials used in Reading Update were taken directly from the state workshops, Ms. Price heard about the reform in ways similar to those of teachers attending the "official" state programs.

Ms. Price described Reading Update as "almost overwhelming." Teachers were given an enormous amount of material and information about activities they could use in their classrooms. Ms. Price said that she put most of this stuff in her classroom cupboard because "it was too much, too fast, too whatever" and she needed time to sort it out before she could use it. Each of the five days of the workshop focused on different reading strategies—what they were intended to do and how to use them with students. For example, one day a presenter talked about the importance of accessing students' prior knowledge about a topic before reading a story. Reading research supporting the claim and showing the difference it makes in student comprehension was cited and participants learned how to do an activity that would help them get at students' prior knowledge.

In general, the workshop left Ms. Price bewildered. The amount of information she received was too much for her and left her puzzled rather than informed. She said, "I mean I got a lot of good information, but what could I do with it? I could give you little facts they said, but it wasn't a part of me." Ms. Price said three experiences stemming from Reading Update were quite meaningful to her.

Learning to Write: Experiencing Policy as Learner

During our first interview, I asked Ms. Price a general question about her experiences at Reading Update. She started describing in very bland tones how each day they tackled new strategies to teach reading, listening, speaking, and writing. But then she stopped and said:

> [One morning] we were asked to write something. We were told there was a cracked window and we were to picture it. I wrote it and then I volunteered to read it. I don't think I even reread it before I read it and I surprised myself. I loved it. I was thrilled. That has influenced me . . . how I want to go about teaching my kids.

Ms. Price said that she had never written much before the workshop, but after this experience she started writing often and now highly values her writing time. She has started keeping a daily writing journal and has recently purchased a sketch book so she can both draw and write. She is thrilled with her writing and using writing to unravel her thoughts and feelings.

The writing experience in Reading Update encouraged her to write so that now writing is an important part of Ms. Price's life. She writes daily and she speaks of writing as a way in which she makes sense of the world. Her own writing experiences have led to major changes in how she teaches writing. These changes were encouraged by Teresa Jensen, the school's reading consultant, who modeled some new ways of teaching writing for Ms. Price in her classroom.

Ms. Price learned that as a writer she needs time and quiet to write and that she writes more when she has choice over what she writes. She began to think that her students as writers might need these conditions as well. She commented:

> I've always felt as though writing was important, but I never gave it the attention before and the quiet that it needed. I never trusted this whole process of giving time for it. I was worried that the kids would be bored.

Ms. Price said that she has made writing in her classroom less structured because of her own writing experiences. She no longer gives students assigned subjects or story starters. She makes sure they have ideas about characters, places, and situations they want to write about and then gives them time to write. Ms. Price described a book-making project the class had been working on all year. Students had to write, edit, type, and illustrate a story and then make a cover for it. In the past Ms. Price said she would have set aside so many weeks for this project and insisted that students finish in that time period. More recently she has allowed students as much time as they need and a much wider range of topics on which to write. She is now convinced that both time and choice of ideas are crucial elements in good writing experiences for students.

Ms. Price's writing experience at Reading Update had a powerful effect on her as a learner and a direct effect on her teaching of writing. At Reading Update, Ms. Price wrote. She experienced as a learner new ideas about writing and was able to transfer, with the help of the district's reading consultant, this experience to her own students' learning. If she needed quiet, time, and choice when she wrote, it made sense that her students would need those things also. Whereas the other in-service sessions on reading strategies presented new ideas connected with the policy from the teacher's perspective—how they might be used with students in classrooms—the writing session made teachers learners in new situations. It allowed teachers to understand what their students might experience if they were to change classroom instruction as the policy suggested.

The power of this experience for Ms. Price supports research that suggests that teachers may need to experience a different kind of teaching as learners in order to enact it (Duckworth, 1987). In-service sessions that give teachers activities to do in their classrooms as ways of changing practice or offer images of what changed practice might look like in classrooms (Kennedy, 1991) may not be sufficiently potent to affect teachers' work with their own students.

It is in her creative writing work with students that Ms. Price's learning from the reform is most evident.[1] Because writing is a meaningful experience in her own life in which she learns about herself and thinks about her relationships with others, she wants to give her students similar opportunities. She talks about creative writing as helping students learn to "read the world around them," to better understand themselves, and to "center themselves."

Ms. Price has students work on creative writing pieces frequently. Of-

---

1. Although Reading Update had a session on writing and Ms. Price thinks of writing as a big piece of the state reform because of that, it was really not part of the reform, nor was writing any part of the state in-service work as far as I can tell.

ten she asks Teresa Jensen to help her plan a writing lesson for her class. She described one writing task in which she and Ms. Jensen took her class outside to stare at trees:

> I said I think they need to know they can read many things in this world. And so we went out and we read a tree for fifteen minutes. We chose whatever tree we wanted and we sat down. Here were all these boys sitting down looking at trees. I was in tears, I was back here with my eyes straining. I couldn't even look. All these boys and they were just—they took a little piece of twig from their trees and took some paint and they sat there. They sat there for fifteen minutes with their twigs dipped in paint and studied the tree, became intimate with the tree to the degree that they could, and then they did a sketch of the tree and came in and wrote, just wrote for fifteen minutes. . . . And Steven came the next day and he said "Wow, did that come out of me!"

Ms. Price talked about many of her writing lessons with the same degree of passion. They are experiences meaningful to her as a teacher and meaningful to her students. She doesn't always plan writing. Instead she spontaneously decides to ask students to write when circumstances in the classroom make it seem fruitful: "So that when I'm working with students and there's a situation that comes up where there's that special moment, I grab it. Whether I've planned writing or not, I grab it and go with it."

Ms. Price teaches separate lessons on expository writing. These look very different from her creative writing teaching. Many of these lessons are part of her social studies and science teaching for which students write reports on assigned topics that connect with their subject-area units. For instance, I observed students working on reports for social studies on people who were famous during westward expansion in the United States. This assignment was very regulated. First, students were given an outline of areas in which they should find information about their subject—early life, education, places they've lived, contributions, and so forth. Then they were given help in transforming their notes into sentences. Finally, Ms. Price gave another outline to help them organize their sentences into a complete report. Other than choosing the person they wished to write about, students were given little choice over how, what, and when to write.

The lesson was typical of how students write when it is not creative writing. This project was very teacher-directed and Ms. Price's goal in teaching it this way was to help students learn how to gather information from nonfiction books, synthesize and organize it, and then write a report.

Ms. Price talked about this being a writing skill that she sees as important for students to develop.

Ms. Price's experience writing a creative piece about a cracked window and the writing Ms. Price now does because of the experience have clearly led Ms. Price to teach creative writing differently. Students have more choice over what and when they write. But Ms. Price's teaching of expository text seems unchanged by her writing experience. Students have little choice over what they write, what format they use, and when they write. Students follow guidelines and do so in a timely manner. This division of creative writing and expository writing is similar to the division of teaching literature and teaching language arts skills. Ms. Price apparently does not feel tension in approaching writing in two ways (as she didn't mention tension between her literature and language skills instruction) because the two types of writing lessons have different objectives. The goal for expository writing is to help students develop their abilities to use information to write reports—an academic skill valued in school. The goal for creative writing is to help students reflect on and learn about the world around them. Whatever epistemological tensions might exist—such as what is writing? how does one learn to write?—do not arise for Ms. Price because the two kinds of writing serve different purposes.

Acquiring Language

Another new learning that Ms. Price associated with the policy was acquiring new language to talk about reading instruction. Although many of the ideas she heard about at Reading Update seemed familiar, they were often couched in terms unfamiliar to her. Ms. Price commented:

> I think I've really always taught this way, even when I was teaching in the 50s . . . but I could not put words to what I was doing before and now I can put words to it.

Some new terms that Ms. Price mentioned were "reading as an interactive process" and "accessing prior knowledge." Learning these terms gave her language to talk with other teachers about what she does. She said it had been difficult in the past to describe to other teachers how she taught and what she thought but now she knew that these words meant something to her colleagues and they served as good descriptors of how she thought about her own practices.

In our first interview I asked Ms. Price about what she might have learned from Reading Update. She reported both learning about writing and learning new language. These she identified as direct consequences of her having heard about the policy at this in-service program. But the third learning that Ms. Price reported from the policy happened over time and she did not talk about it until I interviewed her a year later.

Connecting Ideas

When I returned to talk to Ms. Price the second year and asked her again about Reading Update, her answer was different from that of a year earlier. Ms. Price talked about two new experiences that had helped her understand the ideas she first heard at Reading Update.

One experience was working with a science educator on designing a science curriculum using a conceptual-change model. This experience gave her more help in thinking about how to teach using children's thinking as the starting point for instruction. In this case, Ms. Price said she learned the importance of knowing what children already think about the topics they are going to learn and then planning instruction that builds on, or—in the conceptual-change model—changes student thinking about the topic. The other experience was a book she read about "brain-based learning." Ms. Price said this book helped her understand that the brain was patterned by prior experiences and understandings to accept new information in particular ways. To teach so that children would learn, teachers had to be aware of their students' brain patterns and plan their instruction to fit with them.

Ms. Price connected these experiences to Reading Update by seeing that they all advocate "the need to provide an opportunity for listening to the child to see what's in there and the need to check out prior knowledge." Ms. Price went on to describe how all of these experiences were about "making connections in learning" and "working with prior knowledge to find the value of the child." Although Ms. Price mentioned ideas about prior knowledge and instruction starting with the child the first time I asked her about Reading Update, it was as though they did not really make sense to her until they were reinforced by these two new experiences. Ms. Price commented:

> It's [Reading Update] really just been a part of me now. And it's helped the other things [conceptual change and brain-based learning] become a part of me too. I love it now. I've done my reading differently . . . I mean if I am reading something I will talk to myself about it in front of the kids because that's what is in me and I want to do it more because I know something is happening in their minds. . . . I'm checking in on them more . . . what's going on in their minds.

What is interesting in Ms. Price's talk about her learning from the policy is that change occurred as she connected the reading reform with other ideas to which she was being exposed. Policy researchers write of practitioners' interpreting policy because of conditions or ideas that already exist in the practitioner's world. Practitioners interpret policy through their *existing* beliefs and experiences with other policies (McLaughlin, 1987). They interpret and enact policy because of existing conditions (Lieberman, 1982; Lipsky, 1980). Or they interpret policy because of how they found out about it (Sproull, 1981). Each of these presents an image of policy entering into practitioners' worlds and being interpreted in the context of existing ideological or practical conditions. But Ms. Price's story is one of policies and ideas commingling and mutually shaping each other over time. She makes sense of new policies such as the reading reform when she connects them with other ideas, such as conceptual change or brain-based learning, which in turn she makes sense of when she connects them with the reading reform. At first Ms. Price claimed that many of the ideas at Reading Update were bewildering and the experience was overwhelming, but when she connected what she learned there with other ideas she heard later, the ideas became an important part of her thinking about teaching and learning reading. Ms. Price continued to change how she thought about the policy, making greater sense of it over time, as she continued to interpret the policy through new lenses.

Ms. Price spoke of her learning about and from the policy in three ways: First, she learned about writing both as a learner and a writer and then as a teacher of writing; second, she learned a language with which she could better talk about her teaching; and finally, over time, she connected policy ideas with other ideas about teaching and learning. In the process she constructed an interpretation of the policy that was meaningful to her. Some of the learning occurred immediately—the language, the writing. Other learning occurred over time—the connecting of ideas. Some of Ms. Price's learning can be directly traced to the workshop and to the district's other efforts to help teachers understand the state policy, and some is more diffuse—an individual sense-making process that took place because of who Ms. Price is. However, the main impact of all of these experiences on Ms. Price seemed to be an increasingly strong commitment to seeing students' prior knowledge, interests, and experience at the heart of instruction and the place to start in teaching.

Yet, in her practices, this commitment co-exists with a commitment to students' also learning a fixed collection of skills that Ms. Price frequently teaches through traditional pedagogy—worksheets, teaching-as-telling. Most often Ms. Price can easily fit these two commitments into her literacy practice because she sees them as two separate things—two kinds of instruction designed to achieve two kinds of learning objectives. But sometimes the two conflict in her practice. Talking to Ms. Price and watching her teach made clear some tensions that she sees and some that perhaps she does not see but seemed apparent to me as an observer.

TENSIONS IN PRACTICE

Tensions Ms. Price Identifies

During one creative writing lesson I observed, two boys did no work at all during the time Ms. Price gave them. Their assignment was to think about a scene in a painting or one that they conjured up in their imaginations and then to write a short piece describing that scene from the perspective of one of the objects in the scene. For instance, if the scene were the classroom, students could describe the classroom from a pencil's perspective. Ms. Price told students they could move around and discuss their scenes and objects with each other, but then she wanted them to begin writing.

Like other students in the class, these two boys wandered around the room talking with others. As other students began to settle down and write, however, the two boys continued wandering. When they finally sat in their seats, they did no writing. Ms. Price noticed the two boys and frequently asked them about their thinking and if she could help them in any way. The boys said they did not need her help. After about 20 minutes of watching them not work, Ms. Price came back to where I was sitting and said, "I've got to let them do that and not try to take control. But it is so hard for me." After a few more minutes, the class had to leave to go to music, and the boys had done no work. At this point, Ms. Price suggested that the boys come in after lunch to write their pieces "to see if they would be more inspired then."

Ms. Price said at lunch that this experience, and others like it, are very frustrating for her. On the one hand she wants students like these two boys to have control over their writing and choice in writing, but on the other hand, she thinks it is valuable for students to try to write from different perspectives, something she saw these two boys resisting. So although Ms. Price firmly believes in what she calls "child-centered" approaches to writing, she struggles with what that means in her classroom when students choose not to write. What is her role if not to intervene when students don't do assignments? How can she tell what is just not working and what is not working because as a writer one is thinking about writing and needs more time to actually write? Her own experiences in writing pointed out the value of things like choice and control over time and space, but those things assume that the writer *wants* to write and will eventually write. But what do those things mean when one applies them to students who may not ever want to write? These are difficult questions for Ms. Price and even though her beliefs about writing and learning—as well as her learning about writing from the policy—point her in one direction, she is not always comfortable with it. Her beliefs put her in the middle of a tension between a goal of student control over learning and a teacher's sense of what students should be learning in school.

Tensions I Observed

Not all tensions I noted in Ms. Price's practice were ones she identified. Another example of her facing two competing goals occurred in a lesson on note-taking. The class was learning how to write reports and Ms. Price told me prior to this lesson that her purpose was to help students develop the skill of note taking so that they could learn how to gather information on a topic. She had noticed that her students, when they did take notes, had a hard time deciding what information was important and what was ancillary. In this lesson, she wanted to give them some guided practice.

The lesson began with Ms. Price asking students to read acts from a play on Geronimo and to highlight what they thought would be important information if they were to use the play to write about Geronimo's life. When the students had finished, Ms. Price asked them to read to the class what they had highlighted. The first few students offered text that Ms. Price and the rest of the class seemed to agree was important. No one offered other suggestions or questioned the choices. But in the last act of the play, John suggested the entire act be highlighted.

MS. PRICE: So did Anthony. Would you read the whole thing?
JOHN: Yes.
MS. PRICE: Okay. I guess the first paragraph would help us pinpoint the setting. So that's valuable. It's not essential, but it adds to things . . . . Some of you might have left it out. You'll make your own choices, but those sentences don't help me a whole lot.

The class went to the next act. Jenny suggested that the idea that Mexican soldiers had scalped Indian women and children was important.

MS. PRICE: Why did you think this was important?

JENNY: Because it provided a reason for Geronimo to hate them so much.

MS. PRICE: It gets at motivation, I guess. How many left it out?

BRIANNE: I don't know. It didn't seem very important to me.

MS. PRICE: Okay. We're all going to have different reasons for taking notes. I know people who highlight the whole thing and that's not helpful to me because it seems like then they have to summarize. I can't highlight anything. I need to jot down words that are important. But that's just me. Hopefully today you will find something that is useful to you in remembering information.

The lesson continued with students' deciding what they thought was important information in the play, but seldom was there agreement on what that was. Throughout it, Ms. Price seemed really caught. Believing in students' constructing individual meaning of text, which is what they were doing, she also wants them to learn how to differentiate essential from unessential information in text. Should Ms. Price have contradicted students' suggestions on what was important in the play and therein violate her belief in individual construction of meaning? If she chose not to contradict them, would they learn the skill of discerning important information from text? If she chose to contradict them, how would she decide whose conception of main idea and important details is correct? After the lesson, Ms. Price commented that she had really struggled in teaching it. She hadn't thought that students would come up with different ideas about what was important, although in the middle of teaching, she understood why that was happening. Her final comment to me was that she would have to think about this lesson more.

Figuring out which goal to work for and which pedagogy to use in any one lesson creates a tension. In this lesson, is the individual construction of meaning of the Geronimo text more valuable than the skill of taking notes on essential information? In the previous example, does the value of students' having control over their writing outweigh the possible learning they might achieve by writing a story from another object's perspective? Rather than solving this tension by always choosing one side or the other, Ms. Price seems to manage the tension (Lampert, 1985) by dealing with the problem in a specific context and using the problem as a way of reflecting on her own thinking and practices. She attempts both to use child-centered approaches and to teach more directedly. In watching Ms. Price do this difficult managing, I not only wondered about the tension Ms. Price felt but wondered how that tension affected students. Did they learn about essential ideas in text or did they feel validated in their meaning-making of the Geronimo play? Or were they just confused? Did the two boys feel they had control of their writing and were they really struggling to think of things to write? Or were they just goofing off and hoping to get away with it?

Tensions such as those just described are perhaps inherent in teaching, especially when teachers attempt ambitious practices. All teachers have a variety of instructional goals and objectives that lend themselves to different ways of teaching and thinking about teaching. Throwing into the picture ideas such as child-centered instruction and student control over learning only complicates the picture. Ms. Price has multiple agendas in her teaching and the multiple agendas are not always easy for her to pull off in practice. But what role does the policy play in this tension? Does it offer her any help? If indeed teachers such as Ms. Price interpret the policy to be advocating a child-centered vision of literacy instruction, how should it look in their classrooms? Are there fixed language skills to learn and important learning experiences for students to have, and if so, how should they be taught? There is no guidance in the policy that would help teachers answer those questions.

MS. PRICE, A CASE OF . . .

Ms. Price's case of learning from and about the policy raises some interesting issues in policy implementation. The first issue is the kind of learning experiences teachers might need to enact the policy in their practice. Ms. Price's most powerful experience connected to the policy was one in which she became a learner in the new way of learning the policy advocated. The experience of being asked to write helped Ms. Price become a writer and understand what it meant to write. It helped her see what conditions might be necessary for her students to write well—things such as choice over topics and time—and, therefore, what she might have to do as a teacher to set up good writing experiences. This perspective is often lacking in staff-development programs. In this case, for instance, teachers had few opportunities in the state or district workshops to experience learning in new ways. Instead, most activities were presented from the teachers' perspective—they were modeled for teachers so that they could see what they needed to do differently. Ms. Price found these types of sessions not particularly helpful, because she could not see herself using the activities intact in her classroom. Without some understanding that teachers may need a different kind of learning experience to be able to carry out the kinds of reforms policies outline—rather than just carrying out activities associated with policies—it is unclear how effective staff development will be in helping teachers adopt new policy ideas in their practices.

The second issue has to do with Ms. Price's learning over time as she connected the policy with other ideas. If this study had been finished in a year, my story of Ms. Price's learning would have been quite different. At first, she talked of little learning from the policy. As she said in the first interview, it was something she put in the cupboard—both the in-service materials that were physically put in the cupboard and the ideas she put in her mental cupboard. But this changed as she associated what she remembered from the policy with other new ideas that she was learning. Elmore and McLaughlin (1988) write that policy implementation takes place over time. Ms. Price seems an example of this, as well as an example that *learning* from policy takes place over time. The way Ms. Price made sense of the reading policy evolved as it connected with new ideas she was encountering. These ideas were mutually shaped by each other and, it seems, it was in the mutually shaping process that the ideas gained importance in Ms. Price's thinking. This seems a variation on Kingdon's (1984) comments cited at the beginning of this chapter. Even though Ms. Price was already "doing" many of the ideas and practices associated with a view of this policy, the policy enabled her to make different sense of those practices and ideas. In the process, her understanding of the ideas and of the policy changed. So her learning from the policy changed and increased in the time period I observed and talked with her. Given Ms. Price's reflective nature and her interest in new ideas, it seems that this process of making sense of the reading policy is not over.

The third issue concerns the guidance policies offer to teachers attempting to implement the new ideas in their practices. This policy reform included some ideas about what reading is and the purpose of reading. But it contained little about what that would mean in a classroom. When asked, reformers could offer little help in constructing what a classroom would look like that would be aligned to the policy. Moreover, it did not address at all, either in the documentation connected to the policy nor in the in-service work, how the policy ideas would fit with other ideas about reading instruction that teachers held. How were teachers such as Ms. Price to teach punctuation, literary devices such as cause and effect, or language tools such as note-taking? The policy's silence on these issues means that teachers such as Ms. Price are left on their own to figure out what to do. For teachers to understand how to pull off the vision of literacy instruction the state is advocating, it is necessary that reformers recognize the complexities of practices and offer guidance to teachers to help them make "good" pedagogical decisions given those complexities.

Ms. Price is clearly a teacher who thinks very hard about teaching.

She has taught for a number of years, and in listening to her talk about her teaching, it is clear that her "hard thinking" is not a new habit. Ideas about teaching and learning are serious business for Ms. Price. Ms. Price took the ideas connected to the reading policy to heart and attempted, in a time period measured in years, to make sense of them and use them in her practice. Observing and interviewing her made me wonder whether policymakers take their own work as seriously. Ms. Price was fortunate to work in a district that kept the conversation about the state's reading policy focused for an extended period of time. This was a luxury teachers in most districts do not have, and was due to the energies of the district's reading consultants with little support from the state. Yet even given that, Ms. Price's primary exposure to the policy was to be introduced to new activities and quick overviews of research. By and large, she was left to make sense of the policy ideas on her own by fitting them in with other ideas she encountered. Her learning might have been facilitated, perhaps strengthened, by more thoughtful in-service work at the state and even district level.

The final issue that Ms. Price's case raises is that even though the modal teacher response to in-service work may be a desire for more class-room activities, policymakers must recognize that teachers such as Ms. Price may offer the greatest chance for successfully implementing their ideas, but that these teachers need more effective ways to learn about it.

CHAPTER 3

Tom Fielder:
"I Just Call It Reading"

One of the difficulties of doing this study has been not knowing what to call the subject of the policy. State officials called their work a "new definition of reading," yet surrounded the definition with goals and objectives for reading, writing, speaking, and listening. Some teachers use the terms *language arts* or *literacy* to denote their teaching of the four areas in a connected fashion. When I asked Mr. Fielder what he calls this subject area, he responded somewhat wryly: "I just call it reading."

Mr. Fielder's comment is indicative of his caution in dealing with change in teaching practice. By anyone's standards, Mr. Fielder's reading practice would be considered very traditional. He teaches phonics with worksheets, uses basal readers with his ability-tracked reading groups, and drills students on sight words. He has always taught something called reading and he still does, regardless of the popularity of new language or ideas. Mr. Fielder's traditionalism acts almost like a badge, something that announces the ideological camp of teaching to which Mr. Fielder thinks he belongs. Mr. Fielder calls himself a "dinosaur" and said, "I know there aren't many of us left any more."

Yet despite his commitment to traditional ways of teaching, Mr. Fielder speaks of changes in his reading practice he has embraced because of the state initiative. Mr. Fielder teaches in the same school as Ms. Price and attended the same week-long in-service program. As a result of what he learned there, Mr. Fielder reads different kinds of text with students and uses different pedagogical practices to help students relate what they read to their own experiences.

Of the three teachers in this study, Mr. Fielder is the most forthright about the effects the state policy has had on his teaching. He speaks quite eloquently about how he felt learning about the new reading definition, what it means to him, and how it has altered what he does when he teaches students to read. Yet of these teachers, Mr. Fielder's practice looks the most familiar and traditional and his interpretation of the policy is the most conservative. So how does one measure learning and change from policy? Why does Mr. Fielder construct his reading practice as he does?

MR. FIELDER'S SENSE-MAKING OF THE POLICY

Mr. Fielder believes that the new definition for reading is about reading as an interactive process: "I guess to me it sounds like reading is interactive. You have to bring to reading things that you know to be able to read the information and interpret it." Reading as an interactive process means to Mr. Fielder that a reader's interpretation of text is based not just on meaning embedded in the text but on the experiences, beliefs, knowledge—"things that you know"—that the reader brings to the act of reading. A reader's prior understanding helps him or her comprehend text and construct meaning of what is being read.

Although Mr. Fielder said he always thought of his own reading as interactive—that is, that he made sense of what he read through his prior knowledge and experiences—he didn't use this view of reading when he taught his students to read. The definition made him rethink what was necessary in his instruction: "I'm much more aware of the need to access prior knowledge, because I actually never did that. . . . So I'm more aware of the need to get them involved."

This new insight into how children might best learn to read seemed to Mr. Fielder to have large consequences for his instruction and, as a result, caused him much anxiety. His first reaction to the state policy was, "Oh, no! I've been doing it wrong all these years!" When I asked him what caused his anxiety, he said:

> You just want to do a good job. I picked this profession because it was something I want to do . . . I really love to teach . . . I really like helping these little guys learn to do something. I enjoy seeing the spark and that is why I chose this. . . . So the anxiety was built by the fact that there seemed to be a better way to do the job than I was doing it.

Mr. Fielder's interpretation of the policy was that it presented a better way to think about reading instruction. Although Mr. Fielder associated the policy with an idea that resonated with his beliefs about his own reading, the idea seemed new when applied to how his *students* might learn to read. Like Ms. Price, Mr. Fielder saw the policy as offering both new and old ideas.

HOW MR. FIELDER LEARNED ABOUT THE POLICY

Mr. Fielder reported learning about the policy from four sources: Reading Update—the district's week-long in-service program described in Chapter

2, building-level staff meetings, a new reading textbook series, and the Michigan Educational Assessment Program (MEAP) test. The district in-service program and the staff meetings were specifically designed to introduce teachers to the new reading policy and to give them suggestions for new classroom practices. Mr. Fielder's concern that the state had a better vision of reading instruction led him to attend to these learning opportunities even though he was not sure he would agree with the ideas presented.

Mr. Fielder went to Reading Update to learn "things that I could use to help me implement the new [definition]." To Mr. Fielder, the definition of reading portrayed reading as an interactive process, and the strategies were the activities that teachers could use in their instruction to help students interact with text. These strategies included such things as helping students learn how to summarize information when they read, or predict story events, or follow story structure.

Mr. Fielder said he learned many strategies at Reading Update, but he was particularly taken with new ideas on how to question students about text in order to access their prior knowledge. Accessing prior knowledge was the primary way Mr. Fielder saw reading becoming an interactive process. He said:

> I think what the new definition basically said to me is that the child has to be a part of the reading process. And I can honestly say I didn't exclude children before, but I didn't include them as much as I do now. And by including them, I'm talking about accessing prior knowledge before we start a story.

Mr. Fielder sees attending to students' prior knowledge before they read a piece of text as helping him make "the child a part of the reading process." Students are included in the reading process when they can connect what they already know with text they read and in that way, reading becomes interactive.

After Reading Update, Mr. Fielder continued to learn about new reading strategies during monthly staff meetings in his building. As in Ms. Price's case, a district reading coordinator met with teachers once a month in the building to talk about a new reading activity. Mr. Fielder said he found these monthly sessions very helpful—good reinforcement for what he had learned at Reading Update. He said of both Reading Update and the staff meetings, "It was just interesting seeing all those techniques. There were a ton of handouts which I carried all home. I pull them out every once in a while and read over some of the stuff when I need to." Although Mr. Fielder said he does not use all or even most of the activities he learned, learning them helped him think about what it means for students to be involved in their reading and gave him ideas of things to do in his classroom to achieve student involvement.

Mr. Fielder learned new approaches in reading instruction as well by piloting a new basal series (Harcourt Brace Jovanovich's 1990 basal series) and serving on the district curriculum committee that adopted a new reading series in 1989. A major criterion for the committee's choice of a text was its alignment to the view of reading put forth in the new definition. Although some committee members saw adoption of any basal text as antithetical to the state initiative, Mr. Fielder and others fought to get a basal series that would help teachers, such as themselves, adopt new practices while continuing to use a basal reader. He said:

> So finally the committee came around with some pushing from the administration that we needed a reading series that was updated so that those who don't use whole language would have some updated tools.

Mr. Fielder cited different questioning strategies and a greater emphasis on comprehension skills as the major changes in the new text. Both of these changes he saw as supportive of changes advocated in the new state vision and helpful to him in his own efforts to get students more involved. He also cited longer, more interesting stories as a helpful feature in the new text. Although the edition the district adopted was not Harcourt Brace's "literature-based" basal series, it did contain full-length versions of children's stories taken from published books rather than shorter stories written exclusively for the textbook, as had been the case in the old basal reading series Mr. Fielder had been using.

Finally, Mr. Fielder talked about learning from the new MEAP test. He saw the MEAP as demanding greater comprehension abilities from his students and a more developed understanding of reading informational texts. He commented that with the new MEAP he feels more pressure to "make sure I do a lot of comprehension-type things, making sure students are able to attack an article in such a way that they can get information." When I asked him why he felt more pressure, he replied:

> I never used to feel pressure because I honestly disassociated myself from it. It was a fourth-grade test and I said who cares about that? But, districts are using the MEAP test now as a measure for school improvement. When that happens, all of a sudden everyone is held accountable for what they teach.

When I asked him what he meant by "comprehension-type things," he

said, "More drawing-conclusions type thing, more putting two and two
together to get an answer, rather than just reading the article and saying,
'The dog is black.'"

Mr. Fielder also mentioned that because the new MEAP test has an
informational reading selection for which students receive a separate
score, he has emphasized informational texts more than he previously did.
Primary grade students in particular have scored low on this part of the
new test, largely because of their lack of exposure to expository text. To
give them more practice in "getting information from what they read," Mr.
Fielder said he uses the *Weekly Reader* series more frequently than he has
in the past and questions them about material in it more thoroughly. He
also treats science and social studies text more like the stories in the basal
reader; that is, he thinks about accessing students' prior knowledge about
topics and using reading strategies to help them comprehend the information they are reading.

Mr. Fielder, then, took the state's initiative quite seriously. Even
though he knew he might not agree with everything he heard, he sought
out a variety of opportunities to learn about the state reform. He received
quite formal training in the new definition from the week-long Reading
Update program, with more informal reminders of new ideas and strategies in monthly staff meetings. He piloted a new basal text and served on
the curriculum committee that attempted to compare texts with the new
definition. He attended to the informational reading selection on the new
MEAP test. The sense Mr. Fielder has made of all these experiences seems
to be that the state is asking him two things: first, to emphasize informational text; and second, to teach reading as an interactive process in which
what students bring to reading—their prior knowledge—plays a critical
role in how they comprehend text.

Both of these changes were tied to how and what to teach in reading.
Unlike Ms. Price, Mr. Fielder did not interpret the policy to be a broad
philosophical platform on teaching and learning. His focus was more nar-
row. He spoke of going to Reading Update to find *things to do* with his
students to teach reading better, such things as new questioning strategies. The instructional strategies that he learned were helpful tools for Mr.
Fielder in changing his teaching to accommodate the new state vision for
reading. So even though Mr. Fielder knew that some of his colleagues had
broader ambitions of learning new ways to think about reading and learning from their experiences connected to the policy, he felt satisfied pick-
ing up "new strategies that I'm comfortable working with" to teach
reading.

Given that state officials talk about teachers' needing to "reprogram
their radar" about reading in order to understand the state policy or need-

ing to "reconceptualize reading," it is difficult to know if Mr. Fielder's interpretation of their work is what they had in mind. Is doing different things during reading time reconceptualizing a subject or reprogramming one's thinking about it? In other words, is the message Mr. Fielder constructed the one state officials thought they sent? How would they view the changes Mr. Fielder has adopted because of their work?

THINGS THAT HAVE CHANGED

Mr. Fielder has been teaching in Lewis for more than ten years. He teaches in the same rural/suburban school that Ms. Price does, although unlike Ms. Price, this is the only school in which Mr. Fielder has taught. Mr. Fielder grew up in a nearby town, where he lives with his parents. His mother, a retired school librarian, often helps Mr. Fielder with schoolwork such as designing bulletin boards or editing students' stories. Mr. Fielder talks about himself as a very traditional person who does not buy into "fads" easily either in teaching or in his personal life. Whatever changes Mr. Fielder adopts, they are carefully considered before they appear in Mr. Fielder's practice. He said about himself and other teachers in his building:

> I don't think you'll find anybody in this building who will throw out their whole program and adopt another program overnight. . . . You see if it works, see if you are comfortable with it, see if it helps your students and [then decide whether to] adopt it or abandon it. . . . So you know, the drastic swings that you see in education from extreme to extreme, really don't seem to be in effect a lot here.

But Mr. Fielder has changed because of the new state reading definition. The major changes Mr. Fielder mentioned have been increased reading of informational text and questioning of students as a pre-reading activity. Mr. Fielder has found the new reading series a great help to him in carrying out these changes. The new basal series (Harcourt Brace Jovanovich Laureate Edition, 1990 edition) has informational reading selections in each unit, a list of pre-reading questions for each selection, and a series of comprehension-building questions not only for each selection but across selections within units. Although Mr. Fielder said he learned the new ideas at Reading Update, the basal series "got him on the right track" in using these ideas in his practice.

This was a pleasing situation for Mr. Fielder because he could change in the direction of the state policy and at the same time continue to use his basal reading text as the foundation of his instruction. The most helpful session Mr. Fielder attended at Reading Update was one in which the presenter demonstrated how to use a basal reading text and still teach according to the new state policy—that is, using reading strategies. Mr. Fielder said:

> They had one guy come in and say "I use a textbook and this is how I implement it [the policy] using these strategies." I got a lot out of him in the fact that he seemed to be doing some of the things I do.

Mr. Fielder told me about this session on two separate occasions. He knew many of his fellow teachers were abandoning textbooks in favor of trade books. This was something Mr. Fielder did not want to do. After this session, he felt he could make some changes in reading to align himself with the new policy but still keep an important piece of his reading instruction, which was the textbook. Mr. Fielder thought that the district, by having this presenter at Reading Update explain how to use their basal readers in new ways, was sanctioning his continued use of a text. His feelings were further confirmed when the district finally adopted a new textbook series for teachers.

The areas of change that Mr. Fielder connected to the state policy were greater use of informational text as part of his reading instruction and more, as well as different, pre-reading instructional strategies. Using informational text in reading was to help students better learn to comprehend different kinds of text and instructional strategies were to help them access their prior knowledge before reading to comprehend all text better. Both of these changes seemed substantial to Mr. Fielder.

HOW CHANGES LOOK IN PRACTICE

Use of Informational Text

Mr. Fielder has changed his reading practices since the state reform to include not only more reading of informational text but use of reading strategies to help students read this text. He said:

> I try to approach them [informational texts] the way I do in reading group—to access any prior knowledge they have so that they are thinking along the lines that they need to be thinking so that they can pull out information. . . . I'm happy to report that there are a half a dozen students in here who can read an informational article and pull out information. . . . I admit it has not been one of my

stronger areas, nor was it a concern of mine until the state MEAP test decided it was something we should worry about . . . but it's okay.

On all days I observed, Mr. Fielder had students read some expository text selection and used "strategies" in his instruction. During one lesson, for example, Mr. Fielder passed out *Weekly Readers* that had on the cover a big picture of a tooth holding an umbrella to protect itself from the sweets and fried foods that were raining down on it. The title of the article was "Tooth-Friendly Snacks." Mr. Fielder started the discussion about the article:

MR. FIELDER: Who can predict what the article on the front page is going to be about?
CLASS: [shouts] TEETH!
MR. FIELDER: Good. Who can tell me why it is important to brush your teeth?
RAYMOND: Because they could rot. My grandfather's teeth started to rot . . .
MR. FIELDER: [interrupting Raymond] Okay. What do you think this picture means?
LISA: Junk food is bad for him.
MR. FIELDER: Yes.
DEREK: He doesn't want to get cavities from the food.
MR. FIELDER: Good.

After a few more comments about food and teeth, the class had a discussion about what they could do to protect their own teeth and why they thought certain foods caused more problems than others. After this discussion, Mr. Fielder directed students to read the article to find out if their ideas were correct. He then asked them questions suggested at the end of the article: "Which of these snacks is best for your teeth?" "How can you tell which snacks are good for teeth?" "Did you learn something new by reading it?"

Mr. Fielder said that prior to the reading definition and the MEAP test he did not think of the *Weekly Reader* as part of his reading instruction, yet now he does. Consequently, he uses similar instructional strategies when using it as he does with the basal text. This includes such things as predicting events from context clues and accessing prior knowledge, as he did in the previous example. He does this because he wants students to be better at "getting information from what they read," whether expository or narrative text. So the state policy expanded Mr. Fielder's notions of what counted as reading instruction. Prior to his learning from and about the policy, Mr. Fielder thought of the basal reader as the only text he used in his formal reading instruction. Now he includes other texts—the *Weekly Reader,* the book he reads aloud to the class, the social studies text—as vehicles to teach reading. And because he uses them, for the first time Mr. Fielder uses strategies to help students read and comprehend them better.

Questioning Students

The other change that Mr. Fielder spoke most about was a difference in the way he questions students about what they read. As mentioned earlier, Mr. Fielder said that prior to the new definition, he mostly asked literal questions of students after they read a story—things such as "What color was Dan's bicycle?" or "What was Ruth's dog's name?" He commented, "When I think of the way I did reading four or five years ago, I would say, 'This is a story about so and so and such and such. Which page can you find it on? What can you find on this page? Oh, doesn't this sound like an interesting thing?' . . . and then we would read." Now Mr. Fielder says he questions students about their ideas prior to reading a piece of text—"But now it's, 'Doesn't this sound interesting? And what do you think?'"

An example of Mr. Fielder's new style of questioning occurred with a group that was reading a story about a boy's house. A skill lesson on using pictures to predict a story topic accompanied the story. Mr. Fielder drew a house on the board that looked similar to the drawing of the house in the beginning of the story.

MR. FIELDER: What have I drawn on the board?
COREY: A house.
MR. FIELDER: Is that all?
COREY: A tree.
MR. FIELDER: Right. There are lots of things in this picture. I am going to write three sentences on the board. I want you to read them to yourself and decide how they go with the picture, if they go with the picture. [The three sentences were: This is a school. This is a house. This is a zoo.] Which of these goes with this picture?
SEAN: This is a house.
MR. FIELDER: How do you know that?
SEAN: Because of the house.
MR. FIELDER: Good. Why is it not a zoo or a school?
BILL: Because there would be animals.

MR. FIELDER: How do you know it is not a school?

SEAN: Because there are no kids around.

MR. FIELDER: Good thinking. I like that you read and looked and thought about what you read. And you could tell me why things worked and why things didn't work. What is this story that we are going to read about, do you think?

GROUP: Someone's house.

In this example, Mr. Fielder created some discussion about the story prior to reading it and asked students to predict the story setting by looking at the picture. More importantly, perhaps, he asked them why they thought certain things, such as why it was a house and not a school. This kind of questioning seemed very different from asking students to recall facts about what they just read—what was Ruth's dog's name—because it was asking them to relate what they already knew to what they were about to read. The "answers" were not to be found in the text, but were generated, to some degree at least, from students' putting ideas together. With another reading group, prior to reading an expository selection on pioneers, Mr. Fielder asked students how they thought the pioneers felt when they first saw the giant sequoia trees and then asked them how they would feel. Again, these questions were very different from the literal questions Mr. Fielder said he asked in the past. Mr. Fielder calls them "nontraditional questions," which are "questions about prior knowledge." The purpose is to "get students involved."

Reading more informational text, using instructional strategies with different kinds of text, and questioning students to access prior knowledge are all changes in Mr. Fielder's reading instruction that he directly attributes to the state initiative. These changes have made his teaching look different. Mr. Fielder said there is more discussion around text and students feel more excited about reading than they have in the past. Mr. Fielder adopted these changes in some part because he felt responsible for doing so—he felt some pressure from the MEAP if nothing else—but also because he saw his students better comprehending what they read and becoming more involved with their reading. This last point is the most important to Mr. Fielder. He mentioned often when we talked that his goal for reading instruction is to help youngsters become engaged, lifelong readers, "to create a positive attitude toward reading among the students." Because the changes he has made appear to be helping him achieve his reading goal, he is sticking with them.

But to write a case of Mr. Fielder as a "changed" teacher would be telling only half of his story. There is much in Mr. Fielder's reading instruction that seems resistant to changes often associated with the state policy (use of trade books, connections of reading and writing, integrated teaching).

THINGS THAT HAVE NOT CHANGED

Reading as Separate Skill Lessons

Although he knows that many teachers in the district have abandoned basal texts in favor of trade books and have adopted a whole-language approach (which, in Mr. Fielder's view, is one in which reading and writing are connected and skills are not taught separately), Mr. Fielder continued to teach reading as a series of smaller instructional pieces that cumulate in students' learning how to read. Mr. Fielder describes the parts of his reading instruction in the following way:

> I have my formalized instructional strand, my vocabulary strand which is basically phonics—at least part of it. I do sight words separately so that is part of my vocabulary strand. . . . Then I have the formalized reading instruction which is using the textbook and working on comprehension skills. And then I have my Sustained Silent Reading which is part of my reading instruction. Then we have the typical go to the library and check out books they can read.

These different parts—phonics, sight words, comprehension work, sustained silent reading—are all listed on the daily schedule as separate lessons and Mr. Fielder does little to connect the work done in one area with the work in another.

Mr. Fielder talked about some of these elements—phonics and sight words particularly—as "tools" that students need to learn to read. He teaches these reading tools to the whole class in a very didactic fashion. The teaching is mostly telling and student talk is limited to short responses to questions Mr. Fielder poses. A lesson in phonics I observed seemed a typical example. The class was reviewing the "bossy r" sound. Mr. Fielder started the lesson by saying, "Today we are going to review the vowel families that go with 'bossy r's.' We call it the 'bossy r' because the 'r' goes up to the poor vowel families and makes them make a special sound." He wrote IR, UR, ER on the board and asked Lindsey what sound they all made, to which she replied "ER."

> MR. FIELDER: How many agree? [The whole class raises their hands.] Let's see with some words. [Mr. Fielder writes STIR on the board.] What is this word?

A GIRL: Stir.

MR. FIELDER: What is this word, Josh? [Mr. Fielder writes BURN on the board.]

JOSH: [hesitates]

MR. FIELDER: Use your decoding skills.

JOSH: Burn.

MR. FIELDER: This word? [He writes CLERK on the board.]

A BOY: Clerk.

MR. FIELDER: Good, so we have just proved what Lindsay said. Look at the words, focus on the words, because if you see them and hear them it goes into your brain. What is the word? [points to STIR—one student shouts "STIR"]. This word? [points to BURN; class shouts "BURN"]. This word? [points to CLERK; class shouts "CLERK".]

Mr. Fielder then passed out a worksheet that asked students to circle the "bossy r" words that matched pictures and, on the flip side, one that required them to fill in the sentences with the correct "bossy r" word. Mr. Fielder recited the words on the worksheet first, and then the class repeated them. One student read the directions for each side of the worksheet, and Mr. Fielder reminded them to "use your decoding skills. We've practiced and practiced them, so I expect you to use them." With that the students went to work.

On another occasion, I observed a sight word drill-and-practice lesson in which Mr. Fielder passed out to students two copies of the sight-word list for the week. One copy was on green paper and students cut the words into squares to make flash cards to bring home to study. The other list was on white paper and students used this to study in class. Mr. Fielder asked a girl to read the words in the first column from top to bottom. Before she started, Mr. Fielder said, "Remember, these are sight words. We do not sound them out. We just need to know them." The girl then read the words (*better, bring, clean, cut, done, always, about*) correctly. Stephanie read the words in the second list, stumbling over the word *could*. Mr. Fielder responded, "The third word makes the 'u' sound," at which time Stephanie shouted out "Could!" Mr. Fielder replied, "A little work gets you a long way." Mr. Fielder then instructed students, "CUT!" At that command, students cut up the green copy of the list and placed their words in little bags to take home for practice. A few who were fast cutters studied the words when they finished. Mr. Fielder congratulated them on their good use of time.

Following this, Mr. Fielder wrote 10 words on the board. After writing each word, Mr. Fielder held up a flash card with the word printed on it and asked students to read it. He asked them to read each word four times, moving the card slightly each time so that students had to move their eyes and head to follow the flash card. During one of the flash-card routines Mr. Fielder said: "You have to follow the card. You need to use your voice and eyes to get it in your memory." Mr. Fielder did this for each of the 10 words, with students shouting the words more loudly with each repetition.

In phonics and sight-word lessons, students spent a great deal of time filling out worksheets and doing other written seat work. Every morning, Mr. Fielder puts a packet of worksheets and assignments on student desks. One day these included a worksheet on words that have the u-vowel sound, a letter form students were to use to write Mr. Fielder a letter about something important to them, a fill-in-the-blanks worksheet on cause and effect, and three drill-and-practice addition papers. Students worked on these assignments through much of the morning while Mr. Fielder taught the individual reading groups.

Mr. Fielder said that he emphasizes phonics and sight words in the beginning of the year before he goes "heavy-duty into comprehension skills" in the second semester. At first he wants students to gain confidence in their ability to actually identify words so that they can begin to enjoy reading. Mr. Fielder said he has always taught separate lessons on phonics and sight words as part of his reading instruction and he believes they are an important component. He is even more concerned about teaching them now because he doesn't think the new reading series gives students enough practice in either of these areas for them to acquire them as tools. He commented:

> I think a child needs a tool that they can have control over. It [phon-
> ics] is something that they can use to figure out words by them-
> selves. Another tool would be sight words. This gives them immedi-
> ate control over what they are doing.

Mr. Fielder's teaching of phonics and sight words, then, hardly seems changed. He still teaches these as separate skills to learn, out of the context of text students are reading. Moreover, he teaches them as drill-and-practice lessons to the whole class. Mr. Fielder teaches spelling, penmanship, and grammar in similar fashion—all as separate lessons, all in a predetermined order. These skills are tools that Mr. Fielder thinks students need to acquire in order to read. He said he teaches them as separate lessons so that he can make sure he covers all the skills that are necessary and so that he can present them in the order in which he thinks they should be taught. Although Mr. Fielder knows that there are more integrated, less skill-bound reading practices that other teachers have adopted, his approach is the one that makes the most sense to him.

Recall of Text

As mentioned earlier, Mr. Fielder has changed some of the ways that he questions students about text. He asks more open-ended questions before reading to help students connect what they already know to what they read. But Mr. Fielder also spoke of retaining some of what he calls "traditional questioning"—that is, asking direct questions that have fixed answers. He does so to help him assess whether students have read text carefully. One lesson for the higher-ability group had examples of both kinds of questioning. The group was reading a story called "Jenny and the Tennis Nut." It was about a girl, Jenny, whose father loves tennis and wants her to be a tennis player. Jenny loves gymnastics but does not want to disappoint her father by not liking tennis. The problem in the story is how Jenny can figure out a way to talk to her dad about her likes and dislikes. Mr. Fielder started his work with the group by asking them who remembered the parts of a story. The group responded, "Character, setting, problem." Mr. Fielder then directed students to read specific paragraphs in the story to find clues about characters, setting, and problem.

> MR. FIELDER: Now read the first paragraph on page 169. Look for
>   clue words that the setting is outside. Who can tell us clues to
>   the fact that the setting is outside?
> GIRL: The word fence.
> MR. FIELDER: Good. Adam?
> ADAM: Yard.
> MR. FIELDER: Good job on setting.

The group, under Mr. Fielder's direction, went through the entire story reading specific paragraphs and being asked to find words that "gave clues" as to the details of setting and character. Student responses were all short-answer with little, if any, discussion surrounding them. The point of the questioning seemed to be twofold: first, to get students to read text carefully (i.e., correctly) so as to pick up clues on the story's context; and second, to help Mr. Fielder see if students could recognize such words as *fence, outside,* and *yard* on the page. The questioning did not seem to be about students' making sense or interpreting text.

But after Mr. Fielder and his students marched through the text finding clue words, his questioning switched from this directed, "right-answer" approach to one focusing on interpretation of text. He began to ask questions that were open-ended and designed to help students think about how the story related to their own lives. For instance, Mr. Fielder asked his students how Jenny and her dad started to solve their communication problem.

> MR. FIELDER: What do they do?
> CHRIS: They talk to each other.
> MR. FIELDER: Yeah, very good. So they did something that we can do when we have a problem with our parents or teachers. We've picked up some ideas for our own life through reading this story. What do you think Jenny's dad is like?
> RON: A tennis nut.
> MR. FIELDER: Well, we know he is a tennis nut, but once he listens to Jenny we know that her dad is what else? [No one responds.] I know this is pretty broad, but what do you think? Has her father given up teaching tennis to Jenny?
> DEREK: No.
> ANGELA: No, but he is going to watch her at gymnastics too.
> MR. FIELDER: Right. I think he's a father who listens.

Mr. Fielder asked these questions with a different tone of voice and style. He paused between questions and responses as if he were thinking hard about how he might respond. He allowed some chatter among students so that they could share what they were thinking. At the end, when Mr. Fielder said he thought Jenny now had a father who listened, Mr. Fielder and the group seemed satisfied, as if they had figured out what the story was about after all and they found it pleasant.

Mr. Fielder's questioning, like the rest of his reading instruction, is a mixture of old and new practices. There are new elements—informational reading, instructional strategies— that he has adopted because of what he learned from the state initiative. But there are also old practices—isolated skill lessons, ability groups, basal readers—that he has not changed because of what he heard from the state effort. Given that Mr. Fielder talks about other teachers adopting more innovative practices than he because of the reading policy, such practices as whole language and integrated literacy instruction, it seems impossible to conclude that he is unaware of alternative portraits of teaching. He knows that some teachers in his building who received the same instruction at Reading Update have responded very differently to the ideas presented. Given the serious effort Mr. Fielder put forth to learn about the state's new ideas about reading, it also seems impossible to conclude that Mr. Fielder rejects change out of hand or is disinterested in working to make changes in his practice. However he interprets the state's new reading definition and its implications for practice, it is not out of ignorance of other interpretations or disinterest in the ideas, but deliberate choices of what is best in his professional judgment. Why?

UNDERSTANDING CHANGE AND RESISTANCE TO CHANGE

Mr. Fielder quite frequently talked about the changes he has made in his reading practice as having to "fit" with his more long-standing ideas and practices in reading. He said:

> I teach in a way that is comfortable for me and then I try to accommodate new ideas. I'm not comfortable, for instance, with whole language. I like things in nice little cubicles. I work well with them.

In looking at the changes Mr. Fielder has adopted in response to the state policy, it seems clear that he has been able to fit these new practices — questioning, informational text, and so forth — into his existing framework for reading instruction. He can still use the basal text, divide reading up into "little cubicles," and group his students according to ability. So although the changes he has made in the last few years seem large to Mr. Fielder and have caused him anxiety, he has moved swiftly from the uneasiness he initially felt to construct a practice in which new ideas about how to teach students to read coexist with many of his old beliefs about reading instruction. Although to an outsider this mélange of practices may seem an uneasy one, to Mr. Fielder the different pieces fit well together. Each piece (e.g., phonics, accessing prior knowledge, sight words, textual interpretation) has its own function and can be taught using a pedagogy that best matches that function. Each piece contributes to children's learning to read.

Fitting the new and old together to construct a practice that is changed and yet remains the same, Mr. Fielder's practice raises two questions. The first is whether the learning opportunities associated with the policy were strong enough to initiate fundamental change in teaching. Cognitive psychologists write that learners normally respond to new ideas by assimilating them to their existing schemata, unless the new ideas so dramatically challenge the premise of the existing schemata that they change it. Kennedy (1991) relates this theory to teacher education by writing that teachers need to be given vivid portraits of changed practices that challenge their existing beliefs about teaching in order to shed those beliefs and think about change. Although Mr. Fielder had numerous learning opportunities occasioned by the policy, none of them may have been vivid enough to undermine his beliefs and cause him to question how he fundamentally thinks about reading.

What kind of learning opportunity could challenge Mr. Fielder's beliefs? The policy itself might have guided policymakers in answering that question. Mr. Fielder said that he learned from the policy that he needed an understanding of his students' prior knowledge to guide their learning from text. Yet policymakers provided few opportunities for themselves to understand Mr. Fielder's prior knowledge and beliefs about reading and reading instruction to guide his learning of the policy. Information about the new ideas in reading was transmitted to Mr. Fielder most often using almost stereotypically traditional pedagogy, which provided Mr. Fielder few, if any, opportunities to make sense in an active and collaborative way of what he was hearing. He certainly did not see the policy as action.

And what might policymakers have learned about Mr. Fielder's learning if they had followed their own vision and gained some understanding of Mr. Fielder's beliefs and prior experiences? This question has to do with the scope of learning opportunities available to teachers. Mr. Fielder perceived the state policy to be about reading instruction in the abstract. He saw it as giving him new messages about how students learn to read and what kind of reading students need to do. But Mr. Fielder constructs his reading practices by drawing on a much wider array of beliefs and ideas than those connected to reading instruction. Particularly, he draws on his ideas of how *his* students in *his* school learn. It is within the particular context of his classroom that Mr. Fielder makes decisions about how to teach. Ideas about reading instruction make up only a part of that context and Mr. Fielder has strong feelings about other parts of the context as well.

On every occasion we talked, Mr. Fielder expressed concern about the kinds of lives his children led outside of his classroom. Lewis's economy, tied to farming and the nearby automobile plants, has been hard hit lately and many of Mr. Fielder's students live in families facing serious economic difficulties. Mr. Fielder talks about his students' families being in disarray, parents lacking both time and energy to provide order—which Mr. Fielder sees as vital for children. "I know that my students are on their own a great deal. That this may be the only place they have any decent stimulation. We're working with kids who are very concrete. And they are going to be even more so because we're starting to deal with children who are, for lack of a better word, brain dead because they sit in front of television all the time so there is not an awful lot going on."

Because Mr. Fielder sees little order and adult guidance in his students' lives, he is committed to providing these qualities in his classroom—and he does so very well. I observed one day when Mr. Fielder's students were finishing a Thanksgiving art project that involved dyeing handkerchiefs with natural dyes they had made the previous day. All during the day, Mr. Fielder called three students at a time to soak their handkerchiefs in the dye pots. He set a timer and when the timer went off the students and Mr. Fielder went over to the pots, wrung out the handkerchiefs and hung them on hangers on the light fixtures in the room. This whole procedure, which in many classrooms would have resulted in lost instruction time if not total chaos, was handled very smoothly. Students quietly did what they had to do and patiently waited their turn. Mr. Fielder never missed a beat and continued to teach while he set a timer, wrung out cloth, and hung up hangers. Students not involved in the dyeing process continued to work through other activities. This example is indicative of the kind of controlled, orderly classroom that Mr. Fielder maintains. During all the times I was in the classroom, students always seemed to know what was expected of them, what was going to happen next, and what their responsibilities were. This is no small feat.

One reason that Mr. Fielder does not like many of the new images of literacy instruction is that they appear disorderly to him. Trade books and whole language do not offer a sequential, planned approach to learning how to read. Mr. Fielder said he sticks with basal readers and separate skill lessons because they do present concepts in an orderly manner, one lesson building on another: "I think that a nice methodical progression is very beneficial to students, especially the kind of student we have from many disarrayed households. They don't get any order at home and so they need order in school." Mr. Fielder talks about students' needing order, needing to learn responsibility for their own actions, and needing to understand commitment to their community.

The learning opportunities connected to the policy offered Mr. Fielder alternative images of reading instruction but did not consider other issues, such as social context. Mr. Fielder makes decisions about how he teaches reading using beliefs and ideas about much more than reading instruction. He considers his beliefs about the lives of the children in his class and what they might need from him beyond skills or information. His theories on how they should learn in general seem to frame which ideas about reading instruction he finds useful.

His argument is similar to that of Delpit (1988), who suggests that although new approaches to literacy may be appropriate for some children, they may not be appropriate for all children. And although Mr. Fielder's thinking about what is appropriate and why is different from Delpit's (if for no other reason than that Mr. Fielder is not making an argument about minority children and their relationship to the dominant culture), both seem to share a sense that even though they may see value in the new literacy approaches, their broader commitment to their students suggests other approaches. Mr. Fielder said that if he were to teach in another community, such as one of the more affluent suburbs, he would probably teach reading differently because his students would have different needs. Unless the learning opportunities associated with policy address these broader concerns that influence how teachers teach reading—for instance, an opportunity for Mr. Fielder to question his belief that children from economically depressed homes need order in school—it seems unlikely that they will adopt more wholesale changes.

Is he right? This reform policy is touted as appropriate for all learners in all contexts but does not address what it might mean to teach reading according to the new vision to children of various cultural backgrounds, economic conditions, or social experiences. Should reading in suburban Detroit look the same as it does inner-city Flint? Can children from families experiencing severe economic circumstances learn to read using a whole-language approach as well as children from affluent households? Do children with little adult intervention in their outside lives prosper in classrooms where order and control are less overtly demonstrated? Again, because the policy does not address these questions, Mr. Fielder's answers go unchallenged.

MR. FIELDER, A CASE OF . . .

Mr. Fielder is an interesting case of what it takes for teachers to change and how that change is measured. Mr. Fielder did have various learning opportunities connected to the new policy from which he learned and through which he changed his teaching practices. He went to a reading in-service program connected to the policy, he used a new basal reader, he became familiar with the MEAP test. These opportunities were fairly extensive compared with those of many teachers in the state. But these opportunities seemed to challenge only a few of the ideas and beliefs that Mr. Fielder draws on to construct his reading practice. They did not address Mr. Fielder's concerns about the social context in which he teaches and his beliefs about the experiences with reading that his particular students need. One possible conclusion from Mr. Fielder's story is that changes in reading instruction involve far more than alternative views of reading or reading pedagogy. Unless learning opportunities offer help to teachers in reevaluating their own thinking about the role reading and the role school play in their students' lives and unless they address the particular issue of whether these policies are equally appropriate for all students, it seems likely that teachers like Mr. Fielder will continue to pick and choose pieces of the policy that they see best suiting their own context and resisting any more wholesale change.

Another possible conclusion, though, is that it is not the policy or the learning opportunities that are solely responsible for Mr. Fielder's lack of big changes. Another factor in Mr. Fielder's learning in connection with the policy is his *perception* of the learning opportunities—what he thought he needed to learn and what he thought the policy was teaching. Mr. Fielder perceived the policy to be about reading instruction and he sought out from the learning opportunities available only messages about reading instruction. This was different from Ms. Price, who interpreted the policy as addressing how it is that students learn in general and used the same learning opportunities as to rethink her ideas about learning. So Mr. Fielder's view of the policy seems as much a product of how he perceived the policy's messages as of the messages themselves.

And this raises the question of why learners learn what they do. What role do Mr. Fielder's personal dispositions—his hesitancy to change, his anxiety over new ideas—play in how he learns from policy? Challenging teachers' personal dispositions seems a much more difficult task than changing their ideas about reading or pedagogy and is normally viewed as something beyond the purview of staff development. But it may be necessary to do so to bring about the changes in practice that policymakers envision. What kind of learning opportunities would overcome Mr. Fielder's resistance to change? What experiences might break through his anxiety? What kind of support would Mr. Fielder need to break through his personal resistance to take the risks associated with wholesale change? Thinking about teachers as learners from policy who bring to their learning personal dispositions and habits that shape the learning they do seems important for policymakers. Just as Mr. Fielder considers the psychosocial baggage his students bring to their learning, policymakers involved in staff development must consider the needs of their learners as well.

Thinking about Mr. Fielder as a learner also raises the question of whether the message the state is trying to teach is appropriate for all learners. Teachers teach in ways that seem most effective to them and best suited to who they are. Mr. Fielder believes students need a structured learning environment and believes that he teaches best in such an environment. He has created a very good structured learning environment in his classroom in which students work hard and learn. Even if Mr. Fielder engaged in learning opportunities that addressed his concerns about change, it is not a given that he would embrace wholesale change or that he should. Perhaps the incremental changes that Mr. Fielder adopted in light of the reading policy are the most effective ones he could adopt given who he is. Just as Mr. Fielder sets different learning goals and outcomes for his students, policymakers may have to consider, and applaud, the different ways their learners respond to what they have been taught.

Finally, this story points out the difficulty of determining the impact of the policy on Mr. Fielder's reading practices. To Mr. Fielder, the state policy has had far reaching effects on his practice. He was anxious when he first heard about it and anxious when he first attempted change. Of all the teachers I have observed, Mr. Fielder talks the most about learning and change directly related to the state reform. And the changes he made are important to him in that he thinks he is doing a better job of teaching reading now than he was before. Because Mr. Fielder is so traditional and so suspicious of change, his efforts to change his reading practices should not be devalued.

Yet, to an outsider Mr. Fielder's practice might seem largely untouched by the policy. He still teaches from basals and does separate skill lessons unconnected to the text students are reading. He still sees reading as a series of skills to be mastered before comprehension can be achieved.

From whose perspective do we measure change? This question is important in that Mr. Fielder's learning and change should neither be devalued for not being sufficient (if measured against a standard vision, they probably would be) nor overinflated for being greater than they are (Mr. Fielder's perspective on how far he has come may lead to this). Valuing how hard it is for teachers such as Mr. Fielder to change helps researchers and policymakers respect teachers' efforts and understand that change is not an easy or a fast process. But seeing how much change there might be left to accomplish allows researchers and policymakers to think about what they might do to help teachers change more.

CHAPTER 4

Kate Stern:
The "Good" Teacher?

Ms. Stern is a teacher whose practice would probably please many of the state's reformers. Like Ms. Price, Ms. Stern provides many opportunities for students to read and write text. Sense-making of text, rather than skill acquisition, is central in Ms. Stern's view of reading and writing instruction. And many of the "new" literacy hallmarks such as writer's workshop, author's chairs, and reading companions are part of Ms. Stern's day.

But when I asked Ms. Stern about her awareness of the state policy, she spoke of no learning from or about it. Neither did she talk of any direct attention to it. This was surprising. Ms. Price and Mr. Fielder talked about learning from the policy; how could Ms. Stern not? Ms. Stern works in a district that appears attuned to reform efforts and is known for its innovative literacy instruction, certainly more so than Ms. Price and Mr. Fielder's district. Administrators in Ms. Stern's district spoke a great deal about the state policy and their relationship to it. How could a teacher who worked there and who seemed to follow many of the policy's ideas not know about it?

DISTRICT EFFORTS SURROUNDING THE POLICY

Parkwood has a long-standing reputation for innovation and for a central office staff actively engaged in curriculum and instructional issues. Education is valued in this affluent suburban community and parents have strong expectations for the performance of the school district and their students.

Beginning in the mid–1980s, administrators began a major revision of the district's reading curriculum and instruction. This move was initiated about the same time as the state's reform effort, in part because district administrators were aware of the direction state policymakers were heading and in part because Parkwood's administrators were familiar with the same research and conversations about reading that motivated state reformers. Parkwood's assistant superintendent for curriculum and instruction, in particular, lobbied diligently to change the focus of the district's reading curriculum and used the state's reform to legitimate her own goals. She changed district curriculum guidelines to emphasize reading literature, comprehending and interpreting text, and integrating reading and writing. She banned the purchase of basal readers and reading workbooks in the district, advocating literature-based textbooks and trade books in their place. She also adopted new forms of reading assessment to reflect these more ambitious practices.

At the same time, Parkwood administrators began to advocate a "developmentally appropriate curriculum" in the primary grades. This move centered on the belief that children should be allowed to learn at their own pace rather than be expected to master a set of concepts and skills at artificially contrived times, such as grade levels. Curriculum, instruction, and assessment materials in a variety of subject areas, including reading, were changed to reflect this new idea of individually paced intellectual growth. Administrators and teachers thought a developmentally appropriate curriculum fit well with the new focus in reading. Rather than march students through basal readers and workbooks, teachers were to use a wide variety of reading materials that appealed to individual students and helped them make sense of what they were reading.

Between 1987 and 1992, Parkwood administrators orchestrated an extensive staff-development program to help teachers learn about both the new reading goals and developmentally appropriate curriculum. These staff-development workshops were extensive, not the typical one-day course or after-school workshop. For example, in one of the district's staff-development initiatives participants attended a series of three-hour workshops organized over a 10-week period, with nationally recognized researchers presenting many of the workshops. Workshops focused on both the theoretical underpinnings of the new ideas in literacy (and in the process provided teachers with opportunities to learn about current literacy research) and on new pedagogical approaches that were seen to support the teaching of these new ideas. These approaches included such things as reading comprehension strategies, use of literature to teach reading, integrating reading and writing instruction, using authentic assessment, and using whole-group instruction. In the summer after Ms. Stern's first year of teaching, the district required all elementary teachers to attend a week-long workshop that focused on whole language instruction and developmentally appropriate curriculum in literacy. In addition, district administrators encouraged teachers to form curriculum study groups and make use of peer coaching as ongoing opportunities to learn innovative practices.

Ms. Stern's district, then, is one that supported new ideas about reading that were consistent with the state's efforts and provided teachers opportunities and motivation to learn the new ideas. How did these new ideas play out in Ms. Stern's practice?

MS. STERN AS AN INNOVATIVE TEACHER

Of all three teachers' rooms, Ms. Stern's second-grade classroom *looks* the least traditional. It is one third of a large pod in a building designed to be an open classroom. Although the area is blocked off from the other pods by high bookcases and cupboards, there is much open space and a sense of potential to use space in unique ways. Bookcases overflow with books, and more books are stacked in various bins around the room. Student writing is displayed on bulletin boards. A computer with a word processing program is set up in a corner for children to use for writing. There is a large cart shoved in the corner with numerous mathematics manipulatives and games. Although not large, the room has two good-sized open spaces for groups of students to meet. Room for these spaces is created by pushing student desks together in a tight cluster. Because students sit at their desks infrequently (whereas they spend a great deal of time in the open spaces), this arrangements works well.

Children throughout the day read, discuss, and produce text. For instance, on the first day I observed in Ms. Stern's class, students started out the day writing about their weekend events. They continued writing their "Weekend News" and working on other writing projects for almost an hour. After writing time, Ms. Stern read a book on dinosaurs to the class. They discussed such things as how people know about dinosaurs, what paleontologists do, and what fossils are. Next, students read books by themselves or with reading partners. During this time, Ms. Stern worked with small groups of students reading and discussing a poem. After this reading period, Ms. Stern and students read a picture book on dinosaurs together and discussed the difference between the picture book and the informational book they had read on the topic. They ended their day by reciting together a poem on the joys of reading. The only "non-literacy" event was a 45-minute mathematics lesson in which students worked on place value using beans and cups.

Students read trade books and stories on a variety of topics in which they are interested, instead of working their way through basal readers. They frequently run to the media center, located right outside Ms. Stern's room, for other books to read. The abundance of reading materials, as well as student choice in reading, seems congruent with the state's goal of increasing student motivation to read and the suggested method to achieve this goal. Reformers cite providing "texts for students that are

well-written and have worth or value to the reader" as an important component of reading instruction (Michigan State Department of Education,
1987, p. 6). Ms. Stern does this. She attempts to nurture student interest
and pleasure in reading throughout the day.

Students keep reading logs to record the stories and books they read
and writing folders to keep track of their writing throughout the year.
Writing in Ms. Stern's class is done in stages—prewriting, draft writing,
conferencing, editing, and finally publishing—as delineated in various
writing process curricula, as well as the state's guidelines for writing instruction.

Ms. Stern embeds her skills instruction in texts students read, moving
always from "the whole to the part." By this she means that skills such as
vocabulary, spelling, grammar, phonics, and sight words are taught as they
are necessary for students to make sense of what they are reading. Ms.
Stern gave an example of skills instruction embedded in text with the
book *Amelia Bedelia.* The humor in this book is that Amelia, the children's new nanny, does not understand American idioms—painting the
town red, stealing a base—and so interprets them literally, which gets her
into a great deal of trouble. Ms. Stern said students generally love this book
because it pokes fun at adults and they are motivated to read it even
though the vocabulary is difficult. Students themselves aren't always sure
what the idioms mean or what idioms are, so Ms. Stern uses their desire
to understand the humor in the book to teach vocabulary and idioms. She
sees this as a much more effective approach to teaching these skills than
any separate lesson on vocabulary words or idioms she might otherwise
teach. Often when students are reading or writing, Ms. Stern points out
phonemes to help students decode or spell words. Or while reading a
book to the class, she will point out how she used phonics to figure out
the pronunciation of a word. Normally she constructs individual spelling
lessons for students using words they have misspelled in their own writing. Although Ms. Stern does teach some literacy skills as separate pieces
disconnected from text, most of her skills instruction either is planned
with or grows out of text students read because, she says, "research has
shown that when doing words in isolation, kids don't retain them as long
as they retain them in context."

So Ms. Stern is an innovative teacher with ambitious reading practices
if she is viewed in light of past modal practices. Her literacy instruction
shares many features with some views of the state policy. In that sense,
she is a success for the policy—a teacher whose classroom reformers
could point to as offering a new way of teaching reading. How did she
get there?

LEARNING TO TEACH

The first answer to that question is: Ms. Stern learned, but not from the policy. When I asked Ms. Stern about the state policy, she said she was unfamiliar with it. Ms. Stern had a dim recollection of seeing the reading definition at a staff meeting once and remembered seeing a copy of the new Michigan Educational Assessment Program (MEAP) test, but she did not pay much attention to them. Ms. Stern read the reading definition for the first time during one of our interviews. She commented, "It's what I try to do in my classroom. Getting the children involved, getting them connected to the book." She noted that the policy even seemed to use the same language to talk about reading that she used—reading as interactive, students' bringing their prior knowledge to reading. Ms. Stern expressed no great interest in learning more about the definition. Because she perceived the policy to be suggesting ways of thinking similar to her own, she thought there were no new ideas to learn from it.

Her talk about the policy was similar to other comments she made about learning and changing since becoming a teacher—that is, that there has been little need to do either. In our first interview, when I asked Ms. Stern if her current practices represented a shift in her teaching, she replied, "No, I've always taught this way." Later on in the interview I asked if she had learned from any district initiatives and she again said they had not affected her much because they seemed similar to her existing practices. In the second year of interviewing, I asked Ms. Stern more general questions about change and learning. Had her practices changed at all and had she learned anything new about teaching literacy? She said she has changed her practices only in minor ways—new books to read with children, new games to make—because what she has been exposed to since becoming a teacher has always seemed to repeat what she already knew. Finally, I asked her if she could think of opportunities that would be helpful to her to learn new ways to teach reading and she said, "You mean if I weren't already teaching this way?" So Ms. Stern's practices do not stem from "new" learning as a teacher. Neither the state policy nor district initiatives have had much direct effect on her reading practices or on her thinking about reading.

But Ms. Stern did learn many of the same ideas as those in the policy. The second answer to the question of how Ms. Stern got where she is, is that she learned not from the policy, but in close connection to it. Ms. Stern is a relatively new teacher who entered a teacher education program at a nearby state university at about the same time the state became interested in changing reading instruction. Ms. Stern viewed herself as fortunate that she came into teaching "when the transition was being made from traditional teaching to [a] more developmental, hands-on approach." Her preservice education, particularly her special education course, presented an innovative, child-centered approach to teaching, and Ms. Stern followed that vision.

In her teacher education courses, Ms. Stern said she learned such things as how to teach reading using literature, how to connect reading and writing, and how to integrate subject matter learning around large themes. She called these practices a whole-language approach to literacy. Accompanying this view of reading, she also said she learned how to give reading and writing tasks that children could accomplish at a variety of levels, from children drawing pictures of a story to text with well-developed sentence structure, and how to evaluate student work so that it measured individual progress rather than attainment of a fixed set of skills. This focus served her well in securing a student teaching assignment at Parkwood School (and later an elementary teaching job there). She did two periods of student teaching at Parkwood, first in a hearing-impaired class and again in a "regular" classroom. She commented that these teaching experiences solidified her commitment to different approaches to literacy instruction:

> My major in hearing-impaired talked a lot about language and especially a whole-language approach to reading and writing. So I was kind of directed in that way through my special ed training. . . . And when I did my student teaching [at Parkwood] I did it in the hearing-impaired program and that is the way they do all of their teaching. And I felt that if it was working with those kids, why wouldn't it work for the regular population?

When Ms. Stern did her second student teaching session, she continued to teach reading using a whole-language approach. Because she found this approach successful with her students in both her student teaching experiences, she followed it when she began teaching in her own classroom and continues to do so.

One reason Ms. Stern may have been so receptive to the new ideas about reading practice that she encountered in her preservice education was that, unlike many people who become teachers, Ms. Stern had difficulty as a child learning to read from "traditional" methods. She was in the lowest reading group through most of elementary school and felt, as a child, that she was not a very good learner. When she thought of herself teaching children to read, her own bad experiences led her to seek out alternative methods. She said:

When I was reading in school, it was very, very difficult for me to learn how to read. I think it was because they were taking me about it the wrong way. So worksheets? Yeah, I was worksheeted to death because I wasn't a good reader. So when I was young, I never got a lot of reading practice in school. I was always in the last group to be seen and by that time I was so busy doing my pile of worksheets that I was brain dead.

Ms. Stern's own learning as a child and her teacher education courses stirred in her an interest in teaching reading differently—without reading groups, basal readers, and so forth. Her experiences in student teaching at Parkwood continued to support her thinking. She was primed to reject the traditional view of reading as a set of skills to be learned and her first teaching experiences only increased her commitment. This was more than serendipity. Many of the same people who taught at Ms. Stern's college of education were involved in various ways with Ms. Stern's district. In turn, many district people influenced the direction of the education courses. And both sets of people, district and college of education, played roles in designing the state policy. Ms. Stern's preservice education, the district initiatives, and the state policy were all brainchildren, then, not only of the same intellectual parents—who proposed that reading instruction should be different from what it had been in the past—but of the same physical parents as well. From this perspective, Ms. Stern's sense that the policy's ideas were what she "already did" makes some sense.

So Ms. Stern learned to be an innovative teacher in respect to past practices, but not innovative in her approach to teaching in the sense of seeing new opportunities to learn and change as a teacher. This is very different from Ms. Price and Mr. Fielder. They spoke of learning about teaching reading from both formal learning opportunities—the policy, district workshops, the MEAP test—and the informal opportunity to learn in their classrooms from their students. They both spoke of changes in their practices as well. Ms. Price, whose practices are similar to those of Ms. Stern, said she learns a great deal about her students by listening to their comments on books they read and talking with them about their writing. She sees the learning she does in her practice as essential in helping her figure out what to teach and how to teach it. Mr. Fielder's talk about who his particular students are and what they might need from school also reflects a kind of learning from his classroom experiences. How he teaches is based on how he perceives his students and their needs, rather than a wholesale following of practices learned in the past.

But change and continued learning from either the formal or informal opportunities that were available to Ms. Stern do not figure in her talk about teaching. This is an interesting situation. Has having learned to be "innovative" in her preservice education program in fact stifled Ms. Stern's need for continued learning?

LEARNING FROM FORMAL OPPORTUNITIES

From Policy

When I asked Ms. Stern why the policy did not seem like something she should attend to, she said:

> In this district and in this building we've been doing the reading and writing and so forth for so long, before it was mandated. So the district may feel that we've been, you know, that we're okay and we don't need more.

Ms. Stern perceived herself and her district as being far ahead of the state policy and, therefore, did not see it as something from which she could learn more. But other teachers in her district whose practices were very similar to Ms. Stern's *were* familiar with the policy and talked of learning from it. As is the case with Ms. Price, the innovations in these teachers' practices did not prevent them from seeing in the policy new ideas or new opportunities to think about their existing practices. Ms. Stern's construction of the policy as something old hat was not shared by her colleagues even though many were also "innovative" teachers.

From District In-service Programs

Ms. Stern talked about ideas put forth in the district in much the same way. Ms. Stern started teaching just as Parkwood was getting rid of basal readers and moving toward use of trade books to teach reading. She attended the week-long summer workshop focused on whole-language instruction and developmentally appropriate curriculum, which was required of all elementary teachers. Ms. Stern said for the most part she felt well ahead of her colleagues in thinking about reading instruction and she viewed this summer in-service session as nothing more than a review of her teacher education courses. What she primarily gained from this experience, and in general from all the district staff development programs she has attended in her five years of teaching, has been suggestions for new books to use in her classroom and some new activities to do with students. She did not talk about being exposed to any new ideas about reading or writing or to any challenges to her way of thinking.

So Ms. Stern's talk about learning from the kinds of formal opportunities that Mr. Fielder and Ms. Price found helpful reflects little, if any, new learning. She did not find the policy or district in-service programs to be good sources of new ideas about reading instruction nor did she view them as opportunities to reflect on her current practices. Over the two years that I talked with Ms. Stern, she mentioned books she has read and her master's courses as sources from which she has gotten new ideas, but again, these ideas are limited to titles of books that her students might like to read, games that are helpful in teaching specific concepts, or ways of setting up her classroom to minimize confusion when students move around. These opportunities do not seem to have brought into Ms. Stern's life many openings to think about her teaching. Instead, they have brought new materials or practices to augment what she already does. Because she sees herself "doing" what is being suggested, she perceives these formal opportunities as holding few riches for her.

THE CLASSROOM AS AN OPPORTUNITY TO LEARN

Ms. Stern's classroom is filled with student talk about reading and writing text. Students read books together and they share their writing with one another. They read to Ms. Stern, and talk to her about what they are reading and writing. This kind of classroom environment seems full of opportunities to learn about student thinking and learning. But in talking to Ms. Stern about her teaching and in watching her teach, it was hard to see if *Ms. Stern* saw her classroom as an opportunity to learn. Two examples seem useful here.

On frequent occasions, I observed student authors sharing their work with the class. Ms. Stern had learned about using "author's chair" for students who wished to share their writing with their classmates in her language arts method class. The routine of author's chair started with the student author sitting in a designated chair and asking the class a specific question that they should keep in mind while they listened to the student's story. Ms. Stern said that this routine was to help students listen more attentively and offer more constructive help to their peers. Some of the author's questions asked for help with their stories— "After listening to my story, what do you think I should name the penguin?"—and others were factual questions for students to answer— "Can you tell if penguins fly after listening to my story?"

In the times I observed these sessions I never heard students answer the questions authors asked. Most frequently authors would read their writing, stop and stare at their audience after they finished, and then sit down when the audience clapped—which they always did. If there were comments after the stories, they bore little if any relationship to the questions asked. Almost all of them were generic—"I really liked your story," or "Did you write the story yourself?" Often Ms. Stern would use the author's chair time to set up other activities she was going to use during the day, and rarely did she comment on students' questions or answers. Frequently, Ms. Stern's only intervention was to ask who was the next to sit in the chair.

When I asked Ms. Stern what she thought about these sharing times, she said she thought they were very successful because students got advice from their peers about their writing. When I specifically probed her after one such session as to *what* advice she thought students received, she said advice about how to continue with their stories. I did not press her further (although I now wished I had) but it made me question what Ms. Stern was hearing that I wasn't. Did the comments students made that appeared generic to me appear as something else to her? Or was she perhaps not attending to comments because she was attending to other things? Some teachers assign students seatwork to free up their time to work with small groups or to prepare for the rest of the day or just to give themselves some quiet. Does author's chair serve a similar function for Ms. Stern? How much was Ms. Stern learning about her students' writing or other students' thinking about writing on these occasions?

A second example that puzzled me at the time was a writing conference Ms. Stern had with a boy who had written a story about going to his grandmother's house. This was the first time I observed Ms. Stern and before school that day I had asked her to tell me about the writing conferences she would have that day. She said that most of the students with whom she was going to meet were in the middle of writing stories and she hoped to find out what problems they might be having and help them find their own solutions to the problems. Ms. Stern started off her conference with Ryan by commenting on his opening sentence.

> Ms. STERN: I was reading your book over the weekend and I wanted to talk to you about it. You start off, "Sunday we went to Grandma's house." Normally we want to start off a story with something interesting or exciting to grab the reader. Can you think of something?
>
> RYAN: No.
>
> Ms. STERN: Well, we need a different way to start the story because it wasn't last Sunday, was it?

RYAN: [Shakes his head.]

MS. STERN: It was one Sunday, wasn't it?

RYAN: It was Super Bowl Sunday.

MS. STERN: So you could write "Super Bowl Sunday was fun at Grandma's."

RYAN: [Doesn't respond.]

MS. STERN: Okay? I don't want to rewrite your story. We just needed a grabbing first sentence.

Without saying anything, Ryan took his paper and sat down. When I looked at Ryan's paper after the conference, I saw that he had crossed off his original opening sentence and written "Super Bowl Sunday was fun at Grandma's." He made no other changes. Given what Ms. Stern had said she wanted to do in these conferences, her responses to Ryan were puzzling. What did Ms. Stern learn about problems *Ryan* felt in writing? The conference centered on a problem Ms. Stern saw in the writing for which she provided a solution. How else might this conference have been handled so that Ms. Stern would have learned more about Ryan's thinking and writing?

These examples were representative of the interactions between Ms. Stern and her students that I observed. Although it is impossible to say anything definitive about how Ms. Stern teaches and, especially, how she thinks about her teaching, watching her interactions and talking with her about her teaching made me question whether what students said about their writing and reading altered in any way how she thought about her practices. It made me question whether she perceived her classroom to be a place to continue to learn about teaching. For instance, after watching students in the author's chair many times and seeing little if any helpful feedback being given to authors from their classmates, *I* wondered if an author's chair, at least as it was configured in Ms. Stern's classroom, really was a useful addition to students' learning to write. But Ms. Stern did not mention any doubts about its usefulness nor did she change how she used it in the two years that I observed her except to add another author's chair to the room so that two students could share their writing at the same time. This, of course, meant that Ms. Stern had even less opportunity to interact with student authors during this time. Does Ms. Stern use what her students say in the rich opportunities she provides them as a way to learn about and change her teaching?

Coupled with her talk of limited learning from formal opportunities such as district in-service programs and state and district policies, these questions seemed particularly important. Although her teaching is innovative when considered in light of modal practice, Ms. Stern does not talk of continued learning after she became a teacher. Although child-centered, she does not appear to learn from opportunities in her classroom. Ms. Stern's and Ms. Price's teaching share some common characteristics—lots of student talk and choice over what they read, for instance—but they may be that way for different reasons. Innovations for Ms. Price stem from her own reflection and thinking about practice, which are fostered by new ideas she encounters. For Ms. Price, change and learning are long-standing and important features in her practice. But Ms. Stern's innovative practices are a product of how she learned to teach and not of her continued learning and reflection. Although her classroom may look very different from Mr. Fielder's, she may share his resistance to change.

Ms. Stern's teaching seems a paradox. She is an innovative teacher who hasn't changed. She is a "traditional" teacher in the sense of not changing in her teaching, yet she teaches in innovative ways. How might one explain the contradiction of innovation without change?

THE NATURE OF THE LEARNING OPPORTUNITIES

One explanation may lie in the opportunities for learning. Parkwood administrators mandated innovations rather than encouraging teachers to reexamine their teaching and discuss teaching with each other. The innovations were generated not from teacher reflection but from district directives. And because Ms. Stern already complied with the directives, she may have had little reason to see the district as offering her opportunities to learn about her practices.

State policymakers had clearer ideas about what kinds of practices they did not want to see in classrooms than the kinds practices or thinking about teaching they did want. The main thrust of state policymakers' work was to change teacher behavior away from skill-bound, fragmented reading instruction toward the kinds of practices Ms. Stern already employed. Again, because the focus of state policymakers was on getting teachers to "do" practices that Ms. Stern did and not to reflect on their current practices to see possible differences between what they do and the new ideas, Ms. Stern saw the policy as nothing new. There was little in the formal opportunities that would have created a sense of dissonance in Ms. Stern and, therefore, little to create a need to learn and change.

Although it seems fair to say that the formal opportunities for Ms. Stern to learn about reading may not have been very useful to her, it does not seem to explain totally Ms. Stern's response to them. For again, the opportunities that Mr. Fielder and Ms. Price had available to them seem no more full of opportunity to learn than those Ms. Stern experienced, yet they learned from them.

STERN'S CONSTRUCTION OF LEARNING OPPORTUNITIES

Seeing potential in learning opportunities is a mixed blessing for teachers. Reflecting on practice, learning from students and adapting practice to better fit their needs, engaging in new ideas about teaching and learning, may be very beneficial to their teaching and certainly they are qualities the educational community values, but they are hard things to do and are not often supported except in the abstract. Opportunities to learn may be given to teachers, but time and resources to learn seldom are. As Mr. Fielder's and Ms. Price's cases attest, learning and changing from this policy took time and created anxiety.

Unlike Ms. Price and Mr. Fielder, Ms. Stern is a relatively new teacher. She is also a young woman with many personal and professional demands. She has a two-year-old daughter and during the last year I observed, she was pregnant and having a difficult time. Over Thanksgiving, Ms. Stern had surgery to prevent a miscarriage. She was told at that time that the fetus had been put under stress and that she had to be very careful about getting plenty of rest and watching her diet—things that she found hard to do as a teacher and the mother of a young child. Ms. Stern was also attempting to finish a master's degree in special education. She was pursuing the degree not only because she was interested in teaching students for whom she would need special education certification, but because, with recent budget cuts in the district and rumors of large teacher layoffs, Ms. Stern wanted to have multiple options in the kind of teaching positions she would be eligible to take.

In our conversations, Ms. Stern would talk about her struggle to spend time with her daughter and still have time to plan for the kind of teaching she wants to do. She would talk about how much time she had to spend on her master's coursework—getting papers done that seemed somewhat nonsensical to her, finding time to work on group projects—and how that too interfered with the time she spent with her family and on her teaching preparation. She would mention, as many teachers do, her spouse's bewilderment with the amount of time and money she devotes to her teaching. The demands that Ms. Stern faces are not unique to her. In many ways, Ms. Stern reminded me of myself as a beginning teacher with small children and a spouse starting off his career with all the difficulties and ambiguities that that presents. Certainly many women who teach, like Ms. Stern, are starting off their personal and professional lives and bring those experiences and constraints into the classroom with them when they teach.

And Ms. Stern has set for herself a difficult agenda. The kind of teaching Ms. Stern does requires a great deal of time and energy at a time in her life when time and energy are hard to find. She spends many more hours planning lessons and gathering resources than do traditional teachers who rely more heavily on textbooks and prepared lessons to structure their instruction and curriculum. She spends more hours looking at students' writing than do most elementary teachers. As Cohen (1989) comments, this kind of ambitious teaching is difficult and uncertain. So, putting these two pieces together—that Ms. Stern has many demands on her and that the task she asks herself to do is already filled with difficulty and uncertainty—offers the possibility that Ms. Stern's perception of nothing to learn from state policy (or district initiatives) is in part a safety valve in her life. Learning new ideas and challenging her beliefs would only bring more uncertainty and difficulty into her teaching, which would require more time and energy to sort out. Her practice is going well and her life is full already. She may approach her teaching the way she does because there is little in her world that would encourage her to do otherwise. But again, Ms. Stern's response is one of many possible ones. Teachers in similar circumstances and with similar practices have made different choices—to dig deeper into issues of literacy instruction and to continue to learn and change.

MS. STERN, A CASE OF . . .

Ms. Stern's case raises two different kinds of thoughts and questions for me. One kind has to with researching change and learning from policy, while the other has to do with change and learning from policy.

The first set of thoughts and questions has to do with researching issues of change and learning connected to policy. When I first observed Ms. Stern, it surprised me that she knew little about the state policy. How could her classroom look so like a model of the state reform without her knowing about it? After discovering how Ms. Stern learned to teach, this seemed less surprising, but her story highlighted the messiness of tracing the sources of a teacher's learning. It may indeed be very misleading to cast Ms. Stern as learning from her preservice experiences but not from district or state policies. Neither Parkwood's initiatives nor the state reform sprang whole out of the heads of the respective policymakers. Nor were ideas Ms. Stern encountered in her teacher education classes unique to that program. All these sources pulled, albeit in somewhat different

combinations, from ideas about reading extant in the field—cognitive psychology, social constructivism, strategy instruction, and whole language.
Moreover, many of Ms. Stern's teacher educators, Parkwood educators,
and state reformers formed their ideas about literacy instruction from the
same sources, that is, they attended the same graduate schools of education, were members of the same state associations, and attended the same
reading conferences. Many of Parkwood's teachers and Ms. Stern's teacher
educators became instrumental in the state efforts. In turn, state reformers helped legitimate Parkwood administrators' fervor for change in literacy instruction.

In other words, although Ms. Stern may not have associated her
teacher education, district efforts, and state reform, the three were connected as different parts of the same conversation about literacy that was
taking place among teachers, state policymakers, district educators, and
reading researchers at the time. So to say that Ms. Stern was not influenced
by state policy or district efforts may be only telling the story from her
perspective—what she saw as influencing her. The ideas and learning opportunities that influenced Ms. Stern were shaped by broader ideas about
literacy that encompassed both district and state reforms.

The connectedness of ideas embedded in reforms points out the problem of researchers' assuming causal relationships between what they observe in teaching practice and the ideas in a policy or in a teacher education program. In some policy-and-practice studies that look at classroom
practices without interviewing teachers, Ms. Stern might be counted as
responding to state policy because her practices would contain some
of the characteristics connected to the policy. In policy-and-practice studies that relied on surveys that ask teachers if they had heard of policies or
for their sources of learning to teach, Ms. Stern might be counted as not
affected by policy. Both of these types of studies would probably get it
wrong. The sources of teacher learning may not be that distinct and to
trace teacher learning to one source without recognizing the context in
which that source developed would be misleading.

But regardless of the source of ideas that Ms. Stern originally drew on
to learn to teach, her continued learning seems in question. So another
set of questions has to do with what it would take for teachers such as
Ms. Stern to respond to state policy, to learn more from it. If teachers, like
all learners, subjectively construct their ideas of whether learning opportunities hold potential for them or not, what can state policymakers do to
help teachers see potential? Because many of the learning opportunities
districts and the state offer are based on changing traditional teachers'
classroom practices, a teacher such as Ms. Stern might hear the reform
message as mostly arguing against something she doesn't do, and there-

fore ignore it. There are many teachers in Michigan such as Ms. Stern whose preservice education and schools support innovative practices. Many of these practices, like Ms. Stern's, would fit at least some reformers' visions of what this policy was all about. Many of these practices may in fact be *better* than state visions. What would it mean for these teachers to be affected by the reform when changing their teaching practices may not be the issue? What would it take for these teachers to be affected by the reform if, like Ms. Stern, their personal and professional plates were already overflowing?

Learning opportunities given to teachers that focus only on new activities or focus on changing a traditional practice to the new vision are not enough for these teachers. Part of the agenda of the reform has to be helping all teachers reflect on their practices—what are their ideas about how children learn to read and do their practices support their ideas? Policy can serve not only as a beacon for a set of particular ideas and practices but also as a beacon for reflection and inquiry into practice. For it to do so, policymakers must figure out how teachers can be helped to develop a sense of inquiry about their practice. Part of the reason most district and state in-service programs focus on classroom activities is that that is familiar ground for both the provider and the participants. Helping teachers look at their own practice, giving them opportunities and support to do so, and then helping them make sense of what they might discover is much less familiar.

But to help teachers like Ms. Stern to develop a sense of inquiry and a need to continue to learn more may be a tall order for policymakers. Innovative practices may mask recalcitrant attitudes toward learning and change. What might it take for teachers such as Ms. Stern to undertake these activities? How could Ms. Stern be provided more time and more space, given the financial and political constraints most districts and states face? And would time and space to consider her teaching be enough or does Ms. Stern need something more in order to see learning and reflection as resources rather than as threats? As with the questions that Mr. Fielder's and Ms. Price's cases raise, these seem crucial for policymakers to confront if they are to work with and influence teachers such as Ms. Stern.

CHAPTER 5

Comparing the Cases

The obvious starting point in comparing these cases is to see how the reading policy seems to have played out in the three classrooms. Do Ms. Price's, Mr. Fielder's, and Ms. Stern's practices seem affected by the policy? What did their practices look like before the policy initiative and what do they look like now?

These cases portray images of the teachers' reading practices that were quite diverse before the policy was implemented. Mr. Fielder's practices had many features of traditional reading instruction—basal readers, ability groups, and isolated skill lessons. Ms. Stern's had many innovative features—writer's workshop, literature-based reading instruction, and skill lessons embedded in literature. Ms. Price's practices had both innovative and traditional features—literature-based reading, integrated writing and reading instruction, *and* isolated skill lessons. What is curious about these three teachers is that none of them saw the policy as a radical call to change their reading practices, even though their practices were quite different from one other. Ms. Stern felt completely supported by it and saw no need to change. Ms. Price and Mr. Fielder (Mr. Fielder to a greater degree) recognized some dissonance between what they did and the policy, and changed *some* of their practices, but they did not see the policy as requiring a major overhaul. Mr. Fielder, for instance, did not read the policy to be about whole language, as Ms. Stern did, and therefore did not feel a need to embrace whole-language practices. Ms. Price had some concern that the policy might not support her separate skill lessons, but because the policy said little directly about skills, she felt no need to change how she taught them. Even though Mr. Fielder's, Ms. Price's, and Ms. Stern's existing practices and beliefs were very distinct, the policy made its way into all of their classrooms without fundamentally disrupting them.

These cases present images of practice that were equally diverse after the policy. Because the policy was not perceived as a fundamental shake-up for any of the teachers, it worked its way into their practices to different degrees and in different ways. New questioning strategies were

merged with existing ways of using basal readers. New writing approaches were merged with old skill instruction. So what and how did
these teachers learn from the policy? How did they fit it into their practices?

READING PRACTICES—FITTING POLICY

Tom Fielder

For Mr. Fielder, reading continues to be a series of separate lessons —
phonics, sight words, silent reading, group reading, and so forth. Reading
is first a technical activity in which students acquire certain skills — he
calls them tools — and after that, an intellectual activity in which students
comprehend text. Mr. Fielder says that he spends the first half of the year
focusing on reading skills and only after he thinks students have some firm
understanding of them does he go "heavy into comprehension." The policy did not change Mr. Fielder's basic orientation toward reading. It did
not convince him, for instance, that reading is an act of constructing
meaning of text rather than the acquisition of a set of skills or that skill
instruction can be taught in conjunction with text students read. It did
change the way he thinks about students' best doing the intellectual activity of comprehension, which to him was the policy's main emphasis. Mr.
Fielder says the policy helped him see that students "bring to reading
things that they know" and that it is through the things that they know
that they construct meaning of text.

This new awareness leads him to ask more questions of students. This
is the biggest visible change in his practice attributable to the policy. As
he says, in many ways the policy is just remembering to ask students
"What do you think?" or "What do you feel?" He is especially careful to
ask more questions before reading a text in order to become more aware
of students' prior understanding so that he can use that knowledge to
aid their comprehension. Because the Michigan Educational Assessment
Program (MEAP) test focuses on students' comprehension of expository
text as well as narrative, Mr. Fielder has begun questioning students when
they read social studies and science texts in addition to the basal reading
texts he uses.

The policy has affected the way Mr. Fielder talks to students about
text and has expanded his notion of what texts are legitimate to teach
reading. Prior to implementation of the reading policy, Mr. Fielder thought
of reading instruction only in terms of basal readers; now he uses reading
activities (e.g., pre-reading questions) with many texts that students read

during the day. Even with these changes in practice, which Mr. Fielder attributes to the policy, he has not changed his belief that learning to read is fundamentally the acquisition of a series of skills that must be mastered before readers can comprehend text. Mr. Fielder "fit" the policy into his practice by limiting it to isolated areas of his reading instruction—pre-reading activities, learning to read expository text. The changes in these areas, for Mr. Fielder, seem to have little impact on other parts of his teaching.

Catherine Price

For Ms. Price, reading is not a series of separate lessons, but something that is infused throughout her entire day. It *is* the intellectual activity that children do in school—they read to learn in all subject areas—and so her reading instruction occurs while she is teaching every subject. She says: "Any time of the day, every time of the day, I'm teaching language arts. I'm teaching listening. I'm teaching speaking. I'm teaching writing and I'm teaching reading." Ms. Price reads literature with her class because she thinks that reading good literature is how students get hooked on reading. Through literature, children see the relevance of reading in their own lives. She comments, "If kids are not going to interact with whatever it is [we're reading], if they're not connecting with it somehow, then there is no point in it for them." Ms. Price says the policy reinforces her views. She says the policy made it even clearer to her that "you have to hook" students by "integrating reading with their lives somehow." It also helped her learn how to make writing an engaging activity for her students. She said that before the policy she never "gave it [writing] the attention and the quiet" that she now sees as important if students are to write in meaningful ways. Because of the policy, Ms. Price has changed her writing instruction to allow more student choice and control. These were always elements of her reading practice, but thinking about the policy helped her incorporate them into writing as well.

For Ms. Price, reading and writing have technical aspects that must be taught as well. Ms. Price thinks students need to learn some "tools" such as vocabulary, punctuation, and spelling to "feel good about themselves, what they read and write." She teaches skills in separate, decontextualized lessons, rather than through literature the class reads. She thinks this is the most efficient way for all students to acquire what they need. Unlike Mr. Fielder's practice, however, teaching tools of reading and writing makes up a small portion of Ms. Price's day and even though Ms. Price does not teach skills *through literature,* she often uses other, shorter pieces of text in her instruction. Like Mr. Fielder, Ms. Price does not believe the policy addresses this part of her reading and writing instruction. She says she thinks some "whole language gurus" would not like the way she teaches skills and that she is not sure the policymakers would approve either, but she is not sure how else to teach them.

Ms. Price readily fits the policy into her practice and thinks it has legitimized most of her existing views of reading and helped her expand those views into writing. To her the policy promoted integrated, literature-based reading practices that make reading meaningful to students and help them connect what they read to their daily lives. Unlike Mr. Fielder, she does not think the policy is only about reading comprehension. She thinks its message of making reading meaningful to students applies to all instruction during the day. Yet she is unclear what this means for her skill instruction. She is not sure how to teach effectively the important technical aspects of reading in ways the policymakers might approve. The policy offered her little help in figuring out new ways, so she did not change her skill instruction.

Kate Stern

Like Ms. Price, Ms. Stern integrates reading instruction throughout the day. To her it is the intellectual activity whereby students make meaning of the texts they read and write. In many ways Ms. Price's and Ms. Stern's practices look similar. In both, students read and write throughout the day, using a variety of different kinds of text. Ms. Stern differs from Ms. Price in that she teaches the technical aspects of reading—skills—"in context," through texts students read or write. Ms. Stern says she always teaches skills going "from the whole to the part," meaning that she teaches skills when students have problems in their reading and writing (the "wholes") so that the skills (the "parts") help them solve their problems. Ms. Stern calls her instruction "whole-language," and probably the whole-language gurus whom Ms. Price thinks would be displeased with her practice would like Ms. Stern's, or at least they would like the routines and procedures Ms. Stern uses. Much of Ms. Stern's practice seems to follow the forms of the "innovative" practices without necessarily embodying the spirit behind them.

Ms. Stern made little use of the policy. She was not concerned with it and so paid little attention to it. When she did read a copy of the new reading definition, she saw it as completely reinforcing her own view of reading. She said, "It's what I try to do in my classroom. Getting the children involved, getting them connected to the book." So the policy did not directly change Ms. Stern's thinking about reading practices at all: first because she was unaware of it; and second, because, when aware, she thought it was asking her to do what she already did.

Ms. Stern fit policy into her practice, much as Ms. Price did, by using it to legitimize her existing practices. Unlike Ms. Price though, Ms. Stern thought the policy offered her nothing new. She perceived the policy as a whole-language approach to reading that was identical to her own.

One question that these diverse responses to the policy raises is whether they all fit with visions of practice the policy might support. A difficulty in answering this question is that there is very little guidance in the policy itself as to what it should look like in classrooms. Neither the policymakers nor the policy documents present clear images of what teachers who are "doing" the policy might be doing. One document that gives some indicators of model classroom practices suggests that in such classrooms teachers would use "questions and student responses to guide the structure of cognitive processing in constructing meaning" and would promote "a literate environment by modeling the behaviors of a literate person" (MSDE, 1987). These statements are hardly helpful. What are the behaviors of a literate person and are they same for all? What things would a teacher do to guide the structure of cognitive processing? What does it mean anyway? Policymakers were equally oblique when asked for images of model classrooms. They gave some features of what they hoped to see in classrooms rather than a comprehensive vision for teachers to consider. For instance, one policymaker said she hoped that teachers would "orient their practices toward meeting children's reading needs." Another said she would be satisfied if she saw teachers using longer passages of text in reading instruction. And a third commented that reading should be taught in a variety of ways throughout the day. Like many people seeking to change practices, policymakers were much clearer about what they no longer wanted to see—drill and practice on isolated reading skills—than what they did want to see.

The absence of any vivid models of how the reading policy should play out in practice left teachers on their own to construct their ideas of what the policy might look like. And that is exactly what Mr. Fielder, Ms. Price, and Ms. Stern did.

That practitioners would construct different interpretations of the policy and that policy would play out differently in classrooms is not startling news. Researchers have suggested that local variation in policy implementation is, in fact, a sign of good policy in that it is adaptable to meet diverse needs (Johnson & O'Connor, 1979; McLaughlin, 1990), and have given a variety of reasons *why* practitioners might interpret and implement policies differently. These include such reasons as their beliefs about schooling, learning, and teaching (Sarason, 1982; Weiss & Cohen,

1991); their attention to policies (Sproull, 1981); and conditions in which they work (Elmore & McLaughlin, 1988; Schwille et al., 1983). But these cases point to another factor that has not been frequently explored in the policy literature and that is the learning teachers undertake connected to policies. As one policymaker said, this policy required teachers to learn about reading and reading practice. Mr. Fielder, Ms. Price, and Ms. Stern did learn. But the nature of their learning experiences, what they brought to those experiences, and how they perceived the experiences varied.

TEACHERS' LEARNING EXPERIENCES

These three teachers learned how to teach reading from the same soup of ideas—Mr. Fielder and Ms. Price from ideas directly associated with the state's policy implementation and Ms. Stern from ideas that were closely connected to it. But they all teach differently. What can we learn from what they were taught that might account for their differences?

What They Were Taught

The major source of information about the reading policy for both Ms. Price and Mr. Fielder was the district workshop, Reading Update. This was organized and taught by the district reading coordinators, both of whom were involved in designing the state conferences to introduce the policy. The format and information of Reading Update were largely taken from state materials. The in-service program was a series of sessions devoted to teaching a new reading strategy that would help teachers "do" the policy. These strategies included such things as teaching students how to predict story events or how to summarize what they read. At the workshop, teachers were taught the strategies through traditional pedagogy. Presenters told teachers the policy's new ideas about reading and then modeled the strategies that teachers could use to enact these ideas in their classrooms. A few of the sessions, specifically those that dealt with writing and using literature as reading text, veered from this traditional form. At least in the writing sessions, teachers were taught new ideas about writing by writing themselves. Except for these sessions, though, teachers were taught about the policy *through* the classroom strategies that were connected to the policy.

One of the coordinators of the in-service program said she hoped teachers would take away from Reading Update one activity that they would try out in their classrooms, and by doing this she hoped they would start the process of rethinking their reading practices. She commented:

I have a number of friends who went to our Reading Update who have said to me, "We are going to have fun this year." . . . And they understand what fun means and they understand how to implement some of the stuff. . . . I think people will latch on to one of the strategies and try it and that is fine. Hopefully, someone will show them how to fit that into the big picture. We told people at Reading Update to try one thing, one thing and give yourself five years to feel comfortable with it.

From the coordinator's perspective, ideas and activities were taught. At one level, this story fits with the stories Mr. Fielder and Ms. Price told about their learning at the workshop. Ms. Price commented that she got so much new information that she could not process it all and, instead, put many of the materials away, both physically and mentally. Mr. Fielder said he that he picked up many new ideas of things to try out in his classroom, some of which appealed to him and others that did not. They both talked about Reading Update as giving them new things to do and new ideas to think about connected to reading.

At another level, Ms. Price's and Mr. Fielder's talk about their experiences in Reading Update reveals differences between what the coordinators say they taught and what the teachers as learners say they learned. Their talk reveals differences as well between the two teachers. So even though learning is often seen as a reflex of teaching (Cohen, 1989), Mr. Fielder and Ms. Price are good examples of two learners who were taught the same things yet learned quite differently.

What They Said They Learned

Learning as Learner or Teacher. Ms. Price said the most meaningful learning she did at Reading Update was learning how to write. Although Ms. Price had been teaching writing in a "new" way—using the writing process—for a few years, she never felt as comfortable teaching writing as she did teaching reading. She said she never "trusted her instincts" when she taught writing and was always worried about keeping writing assignments moving along. Before her experience at Reading Update she said that she "never trusted this whole process of giving time for it [writing]. . . . [She] was worried that kids would be bored." In the in-service writing session, Ms. Price learned about writing by actually writing. She was asked to write about a broken window in any way she wanted and then to share what she wrote with her group. She found that experience very moving—she had never before thought of herself as able to write, nor had she ever received peer feedback on her writing. The experience led her to write more in her own life. Writing became for Ms. Price an important way to experience the world and she wanted her students to understand this as well. Because Ms. Price was asked to be a learner in the writing session—was asked to write herself—and because of what that experience generated in her own life, Ms. Price learned what might be necessary in her classroom if she were to give her students the same kind of experience with writing she had. She learned that where she wrote, what she wrote about, and how much time she had to write contributed to the quality of her writing. In her in-service experience Ms. Price learned about writing not by watching a teacher demonstrate how to teach "according to the policy" but by experiencing the policy as a learner. She translated her experience into her teaching practice so that she could help her children learn how to write better.

In contrast, Ms. Stern did not learn about writing from any in-service program connected with the policy. In fact, she never mentioned writing as a part of the state policy. She said she learned how to teach writing in her preservice education courses in which she was taught how to set up a writing workshop in her class. She learned about the writing process, about peer feedback, and about evaluating students' writing in diverse ways. But she was taught these things from the teacher's perspective— that is, the practices a teacher engages in when teaching a writing workshop. Ms. Stern was not given opportunities to experience what it might mean to be the kind of writer she was teaching her students to be. When I asked Ms. Stern if she ever wrote, she said that the only writing she does, outside of letters, is writing her church bulletin. This is largely a matter of compiling notes that various people give her and writing them up in time to meet a deadline. In other words, it is largely a technical activity in which things such as pre-reading activities, choice of topics, time, and environment for writing would make little difference. Ms. Stern does not think of herself as a writer and does not write, as Ms. Price does, on any routine basis.

So Ms. Stern's and Ms. Price's learning experiences with writing are very different. Ms. Price learned how to be a writer and, because of that, developed some understanding of what it is her students might experience when they write in her classroom. Ms. Stern just learned how to teach writing.

Mr. Fielder learned new ideas *as a teacher* as well. He said, "I went to Reading Update . . . looking for things that I could use to help me implement the new strategies. . . . Like today, when I was reading from *The Boxcar Children* . . . that was a think-aloud strategy. And let's see, Read React. I've done that this year." Mr. Fielder said he learned the most in sessions that introduced him to classroom strategies and then modeled them for him. The most meaningful learning Mr. Fielder did was in a session on pre-reading strategies that gave him information on how to question students prior to reading a text so that they could more effectively comprehend the text. The session was important to him because it gave him new activities that he could use with his basal reader to help him teach the way he now thought was valuable.

Given that some researchers suggest it is difficult for teachers to teach in ways they themselves have never learned (Brown, 1991; Cohen, 1989), the difference in learning experiences connected to the policy that Ms. Stern and Mr. Fielder had compared with those of Ms. Price seems important. Mr. Fielder did not learn new reading strategies as a reader and Ms. Stern did not learn how to write as a writer. Both learned different ways to teach students how to read and write without learning how their teaching might be experienced by their students. What does it mean for a learner to have "prior knowledge accessed" before reading a story? How does talking about written text affect what one writes? Ms. Stern and Mr. Fielder could not answer these questions from the learner's perspective.

Ms. Price too was taught how to teach reading strategies, but said she did not learn them. Unlike Mr. Fielder and Ms. Stern, she found learning about new ways to teach from a teacher's perspective "bewildering." Instead, she learned new ways to teach writing by experiencing those new ways as a learner. This was unusual. Most learning opportunities connected to the policy did not play out so teachers became students of the new instruction it envisioned. Even those that did encourage teachers to become students, such as this writing in-service session, were not construed by all teachers as opportunities to learn in new ways. Mr. Fielder had the same opportunity to learn as Ms. Price—he attended the same in-service session—but he perceived it quite differently. The opportunity to experience "new ideas" as a learner is in part given to teachers by making available to them learning experiences that encourage them to become learners. But it is also in part taken by teachers who construe these opportunities to learn in new ways as valuable and important.

Learning New Language

Ms. Price also talked about acquiring new language from Reading Update, which gave her a way to talk about what she already believed. The idea that "reading is an interactive process" helped her articulate her belief that reading was made meaningful for students by connecting what they read with experiences in their lives. "Activating students' prior knowledge" helped her communicate her beliefs that instruction had to start with students' existing understandings. Ms. Price said that she had always believed in these ideas, but the policy gave her "words [for] what I was doing . . . now I can put words to it." She found these words helpful in communicating her thoughts to other teachers—something that in the past had been difficult for her. Although this language at first just seemed to give her labels for her existing thinking and beliefs, later she said that the language she learned at Reading Update helped her to connect the policy's ideas with other new ideas she was encountering because all used the same words. She said, "Everything I'm learning is about prior knowl- edge," so that when she came across that phrase in her reading in-service session, her science curriculum work, and books about children's learning she put all of these experiences together. In doing so, she understood them better. She commented, "I didn't own the phrase before, but now I do."

Ms. Price's talk about the language of the policy is important because it is through the similarities in language in various initiatives that she was able to connect ideas. And by connecting ideas from various sources, Ms. Price made sense of them. This sense that language not only identifies thoughts but shapes them is not a new idea. Mead (1934) wrote: "Lan- guage does not simply symbolize a situation or object which is already there in advance; it makes possible the existence or the appearance of the situation or object" (p. 78). Bruner (1990) summarizes Vygotsky's view of language not just as "narrative or label but as a system of cutting up the world into categories and relations" (p. 158). For Ms. Price, the language shaped a category of learning in which she could then fit many of the new ideas she was encountering. So the language seems to have played a greater role in her thinking about the reading policy than her talk about it might indicate. Ms. Price's learning from the language is also interesting in comparison with Ms. Stern's talk about the policy's language. Whereas the language was new for Ms. Price, it was familiar to Ms. Stern. She said that she had learned all about "prior knowledge" and "reading as inter- active" and "integrated instruction" in her preservice education courses. Ms. Stern's comments suggest that the familiarity of the policy's language contributed to her sense that there was nothing new to learn from it.

If indeed some other language had been used to communicate the same ideas, it is possible that Ms. Stern would have interpreted the policy as offering an opportunity to learn something new. If so, this is something of a conundrum for policymakers, for, on the one hand, the commonness of language (i.e., the fact that it was not unique to the policy but used in the broader community) helped Ms. Price learn and connect ideas so that she made greater sense of them. But, on the other hand, it may have masked for Ms. Stern differences that actually existed between her think- ing and that of the policymakers. If language is not just attaching labels to ideas but rather the shaping of ideas, then the language used to communicate ideas in a policy will influence how teachers learn from policy and what sense they make of it. But because teachers attach different meanings to the same words, exactly how language shapes their thinking will vary with the individual teacher.

Mr. Fielder mentioned the same language as Ms. Price and Ms. Stern in connection to the policy—reading as an interactive process, student's prior knowledge—yet his use of these words seems quite different from that of the others. Whereas Ms. Price connected these words in some big picture about learning, Mr. Fielder restricted them to a picture of reading instruction, such as helping children understand text better by accessing their prior knowledge. To Mr. Fielder, interaction and prior knowledge are tools to do better this thing called reading comprehension. Mr. Fielder related a story about the policy's language:

> I think we talked last time that the one thing that stuck with me from the state's thing [policy] is that reading is interactive. So I try to make it interactive, not passive. My brother and I were driving to Detroit to take my mom shopping. He is not an educator and he was talking about how you have to get people interested in what they are reading and blah, blah, blah. We're going 65 miles per hour down the highway and I just said "It's called accessing prior knowledge and we're now doing it."

So the language that Mr. Fielder associated with the policy may also have shaped his thinking and allowed him to cut up the world in new categories, but the world he cuts up is quite different from Ms. Price's. To Mr. Fielder the policy deals with the domain of reading instruction, perhaps even more narrowly with reading comprehension, not learning and teaching in general.

Mr. Fielder and Ms. Price talk differently about what they learned at Reading Update. Ms. Price learned about writing and Mr. Fielder learned about using basal readers in new ways. Through the policy's language, Ms. Price connected her learning from Reading Update with other ideas about how children learn and in the process honed her ideas about learning and teaching generally, not just learning how to read. Mr. Fielder saw the policy as about teaching reading and therefore learned about reading instruction. When we think about children learning in schools, it seems obvious that as learners they take away different messages from what they are taught. One explanation for this is that they bring different resources to their learning (Bowles & Gintis, 1976; Giroux, 1983; Heath, 1982). The reading policy itself is based on a view of learning in which who the learner is—his or her experiences, beliefs, ideas—affects the meaning he or she constructs. Although learners may be taught the same ideas and information, who they are will affect what sense they make of it—that is, it will affect what they learn. Another way to understand differences in Mr. Fielder's, Ms. Price's, and Ms. Stern's learning is to look at who they are and what understandings and experiences with reading they bring to their learning of the policy.

WHAT THEY BROUGHT TO THEIR LEARNING EXPERIENCES

Mr. Fielder thinks of himself as a person who has not ventured far from things that are familiar to him, both professionally and personally. He went to a nearby college, has spent his teaching career in one school, and lives with his parents in the family home. Mr. Fielder talks poignantly about his choice to be the caretaker of his parents and how this, on the one hand, gives him stability and consistency, but, on the other, limits his possible life choices. He told me a revealing story when a group in his class read a story about playing dominoes. Mr. Fielder told the group a great deal about the game that was not in the story and played a number of games with them. I commented later that he seemed to be quite expert at dominoes and he said that every summer evening for most of his life he has played the game with his father on the porch, even though he said he hates dominoes. As a child he tried to hide them from his father so they would do something else, but he added, "What can you do?" For Mr. Fielder, past experiences and relationships have great meaning. Although he may feel ambivalent about them, the sense of coherence and stability that they provide are valuable to him.

He chooses to teach in many of the same ways that he remembers his teachers teaching. Mr. Fielder talked a great deal about needing to be comfortable in the way he teaches, needing things to feel familiar, and needing any new ideas about teaching to fit with his existing practices and beliefs. He said about Reading Update, for instance, that he was looking for new ideas that fit "within the framework that I'm comfortable working in." This does not seem to mean that he avoids new ideas. Mr. Fielder attends numerous staff-development programs on a wide variety of topics, but he carefully considers any new idea he encounters. Because of this, when he first heard about the reading policy it made him anxious. He thought the state was telling him that there was a better way to teach reading and that something in the messages he heard about the policy led him to think they might be right.

His anxiety pushed him to attend the district's reading in-service program and some of what he heard there made sense. He learned that he should question students differently so that he could access their prior knowledge to help them comprehend new text more effectively. This change in practice seemed dramatic to Mr. Fielder, but it also was one that he could adopt without having to upset his whole way of thinking about reading instruction. He did not view what he learned about the policy as asking him to give up separate phonics instruction, for instance, or ability grouping in reading. In other words, although the change in questioning was a big change, it did not challenge Mr. Fielder's fundamental beliefs about how to teach reading. He made sense of what he learned and used it in his classroom by fitting it with existing practices, not overthrowing them.

As a learner, what Mr. Fielder seems to have brought to his learning experiences with the policy is a desire to know more about it and an openness to thinking about new practices, counterbalanced by a desire to have the new ideas fit with existing practices. And his existing practices are quite traditional, according to Mr. Fielder's own account. To fit these three things together—need for familiarity, traditional practice, and the policy—it makes sense that Mr. Fielder would see the policy as an opportunity to learn about changes in reading instruction rather than a wholesale change in thinking about learning or teaching. His personal disposition not to engage in large changes, or in any changes very easily, would not favor a larger, more radical reading of the policy.

Ms. Stern's not seeing opportunities to learn in the policy may equally be tied to who she is as a learner. Like Mr. Fielder, Ms. Stern brought things to her learning that worked against her seeing the policy as anything but congruent with what she currently did. Ms. Stern already had many "new ideas" in her practice, which make her practice fall into the category generally called "ambitious." She does not use a basal reader but finds trade books for students to read that she thinks will interest them more. She teaches skills through their reading when students need the skill to figure out a problem in their reading or writing. She allows students to develop at their own pace, rather than pushing them all to master concepts in a predetermined time period. All of these practices require Ms. Stern to deal with greater uncertainty over what and how her students are learning than if she followed more traditional practices.

For Ms. Stern to see the policy as another learning opportunity would open her up to the possibility of more uncertainty and challenge. And Ms. Stern may not want that. Her life is already complex with a young daughter, a difficult pregnancy, a master's degree program. Because her practices seem to work for her and because she receives little pressure to change from her district, there is little reason for Ms. Stern to think of herself as needing to learn more. Interpreting the policy as nothing new allows Ms. Stern *not to have to* learn from it.

This contrasts with Ms. Price, who both professionally and personally has engaged in great changes. Ms. Price left home at 18 to become a nun and later left her religious order and got married. She speaks of making these changes in her life because she learned new things and wanted new experiences. For example, Ms. Price talked about her decision to teach in public schools instead of continuing in private ones as important "for her own growth," to help her experience teaching in a different, less homogenous environment. Unlike Mr. Fielder, who appears to need familiarity, Ms. Price seems to seek change because it contributes to new understandings of herself.

Since she began teaching in the 1950s, Ms. Price has experimented with what she calls various forms of child-centered teaching. Although always having child-centeredness as a guiding principle, Ms. Price talks of changing her practice continually to incorporate new ideas she encounters and to meet the needs of new children. She saw the reading policy as similar to what she already believed and did, yet she still viewed it as an opportunity to learn more. And she did learn. She learned about herself as a writer, which led her to think about different ways to teach writing. Initially she found much of what else she learned in the reading in-service program useless because it offered her only activities. But as she continued thinking about what she learned and connecting it to various other experiences she was having, she found the experiences she had at Reading Update more meaningful. What the reading policy ultimately gave to her was a new way to think about her beliefs and a deeper understanding of how her beliefs, as well as other ideas she was encountering, fit into a broad picture of learning and teaching.

As a learner, then, Ms. Price loves to engage big ideas. What she learns becomes meaningful to her when she can see how it relates to other things she is thinking about and when she can paint a coherent picture of all the new information and ideas she encounters. Her disposition is one that seeks new ideas and engages in change. Seeing the policy as an opportunity to examine her own thinking and to connect it to other ideas fits into this picture.

Writing about personal dispositions and characteristics of Mr. Fielder, Ms. Price, and Ms. Stern is tricky. What I know about their lives is limited and my ability to make sense of what they tell me is even more limited. That is not the intent here. But thinking about who these teachers are as people is inescapable because what they bring to their learning plays a part in how and if they perceive the policy as an opportunity to learn. Regardless of what they were taught about the policy, the way these teachers perceived the opportunity was what shaped their learning. And their differing perceptions of the policy offer possible explanations for why they make sense of the policy in their practices differently, even though in Mr. Fielder and Ms. Price's cases in particular, many of the factors cited by researchers as influencing teachers' interpretations (e.g., working conditions, exposure to the policy) were the same.

Bruner (1990), when writing about how people's perceptions of the world are related to their desires and beliefs, uses the examples of some people perceiving the Sahara as something to cross on foot or the Atlantic as something to cross in a small boat (p. 40). It is not having stronger feet or being more adaptable to living in water that produces these different perceptions, but something in the people that creates a sense of deserts and oceans as opportunities rather than as barriers. It is not just what learning opportunities are available to teachers that affects their learning from policy and ultimately their interpretations of policy. Teachers subjectively construct the opportunities and see them as either full of potential or as barren. And the sense they make of the learning opportunities relates to the sense they make of the policy and shapes how the policy plays out in their practices.

This may be something of a chicken-and-egg story. The learning teachers think they need to engage in may be shaped by their interpretation of the policy while at the same time their interpretation of the policy may be shaped by the learning they do. For example, in Reading Update, did Mr. Fielder focus on learning classroom strategies because he thought that was what the policy was about? Did he learn about classroom strategies at the in-service session and therefore think that that was what the policy was about? Did Ms. Price learn about writing and, therefore, connect it to the policy, or did she think the policy was about writing because she felt uneasy about her writing instruction and actively sought out an opportunity to learn about writing? Ms. Stern perceived there to be no learning opportunities available to her connected with the policy. She said she only briefly heard about the policy in her district meetings and not at all through other sources, yet other teachers in her school and district were very familiar with the policy and spoke of discussions with principals and district administrators about it. Did Ms. Stern interpret the policy to be what she already did and so ignored any mention of it? Or because there was little mention of it, did Ms. Stern assume it advocated a view of reading she already held and therefore was beside the point?

These are obviously rhetorical questions whose aim is not to ferret out truth. Lively (1984), through one of her characters, muses about truth:

> He remembered as a small boy, being exhorted to tell the truth; at that point one had been given the impression that this was a perfectly simple matter—you did not say that things had happened which had not, neither did you say

that things which had not happened had. What was not explained was the wealth of complexity surrounding this basic maxim. (p. 21)

Certainly the complexity in these cases is rich. It is made even richer by the fact that the policy itself is vague — the "truth" of it was constructed differently by different policymakers at different times in the policy history. Establishing the "truth" seems neither possible, nor the point. The importance is that learning connected to policy has two facets that must be understood. One is an external analysis or understanding of what might have been available to teachers to learn about the policy and how the nature of it might affect what it is teachers learn about and from the policy. But the other is how teachers perceive these opportunities, and it is the latter that seems to interact with teachers' interpretations and sense of change.

This way of thinking about teachers' learning from policies is not often mentioned. For example, McDonnell and Elmore (1987) write about learning as capacity-building, which in its worst characterization presents learning as a reflection of what is taught and as a uniform event in which all learners learn the same thing: Policymakers or their ambassadors teach information to build teachers' intellectual capacities to enact policies and all teachers learn and use the information in the same way. The learning connected to the policy is meant to create uniform practices. Enacting and implementing this policy did not create more uniform practices nor did Mr. Fielder, Ms. Stern, and Ms. Price learn the same things from it. The teachers as learners, like all learners, constructed their own meaning of what they were taught. They acted, in fact, as the policy said they would act, "reading" the policy in a dynamic interaction among their prior understandings, the policy's messages, and the context in which they were taught.

If teachers are learners from policy, then policymakers are teachers. In this role, policymakers face the same tensions that all teachers do. They alternate between a desire to transmit certain information and ideas to their students and the recognition that their students will construct their own meaning of whatever information and ideas are taught. In our educational culture, both sides of the tension are valued. Learners are expected to acquire some set of fixed ideas and information. Policymakers in this case sought to change reading instruction in a particular direction by giving teachers new information and ideas about reading. At the same time, learners are encouraged to make of the ideas what they will so that a plurality of ideas and opinions exist. Even the most naive of policymakers in this case knew that teachers would take what they learned connected to the policy and play it out in their classrooms in different ways. By casting the policy into the educational waters, policymakers introduced another set of ideas that would be construed to mean many different things. So in an attempt to refocus reading instruction around a certain set of ideas, they may have actually opened up the possibility for greater diversity in what happens in classrooms during reading time.

CHAPTER 6

Conclusions

It is interesting looking at the issue of teacher learning from a policy that is itself about learning. One reading of the policy is that it assumes a constructivist view of learning: Readers construct their own meaning of text based on their prior knowledge (what they bring to their reading), the context in which they are reading, and the text itself. This reading of the policy suggests that readers—learners—will learn various things from text because they will construct different meanings from it. This reading of the policy suggests that learners *of the policy* will construct various meanings of it.

In contrast to the policy's view of learning is the view of learning policymakers assumed in their efforts to teach teachers about the policy. In-service sessions on the policy were taught with traditional pedagogy—presenters told teachers about new ideas and activities, which they expected teachers to "learn" and incorporate intact into their classrooms. The Michigan Educational Assessment Program (MEAP) test was designed to "drive" instruction in that teachers would hear "the message" and change their instruction accordingly. The view of teaching and learning that was embodied in what policymakers did connected to the policy is classic "knowledge reproduction." Learners were viewed as empty vessels that policymakers, as teachers, could fill with new, "correct" ideas (Jackson, 1986).

Viewing their policy as text that readers would interpret in various ways and then implement in various ways would have been quite troublesome for policymakers. They thought they finally knew the right way to teach reading and they wanted teachers in the state to learn it. So what do these teachers' stories say about how and what they learned from and about the policy? Did they do what policymakers said they would do as learners, or did they do what policymakers wanted them to do? Finally, what might policymakers learn from answers to these questions?

HOW AND WHAT TEACHERS LEARNED FROM AND ABOUT THE POLICY

At one level, these stories show that these teachers learned different things depending on who they were and what they knew previously. This sounds like a fairly simplistic statement in line with the constructivist reading of the policy. Ms. Price, Mr. Fielder, and Ms. Stern knew different things about reading and reading instruction and they did different things in their reading practices. Mr. Fielder viewed reading as a series of skills students need to learn prior to being able to comprehend text. He thought the best way to teach these skills was in a methodical, organized way with separate lessons for phonics, vocabulary, and sight words. His views led him to reject much of what he heard about new ways of teaching reading, particularly whole-language approaches. Ms. Stern and Ms. Price, on the other hand, embraced many of the new ideas. They both said they taught reading throughout the day as part of their instruction in different subject areas. They read literature with their students and orchestrated many opportunities during the day for students to read and write. The major difference between Ms. Stern and Ms. Price was in their teaching of skills. Ms. Stern believed skills should and could be taught when students needed them to make sense of text whereas Ms. Price was less convinced that teaching skills when they arise in student work was either wise or efficient.

The differences among the teachers meant that they brought different ideas and practices to their learning from the policy—different "prior knowledge"—which influenced how and what they learned from it. But their stories point out that saying learners learn differently depending on their prior knowledge and experiences is actually saying something very complex, because figuring out what a learner's prior knowledge is, as well as how it shapes his or her learning, is difficult. Ms. Stern and Ms. Price brought similar ideas about reading and reading practices to their learning about the policy, yet they learned very different things from it. This seems to be so because in addition to their beliefs about reading and reading practices, they brought different dispositions toward learning. Ms. Price brought an eagerness to see the policy as something else from which to learn and she did learn new ideas from it—about writing, about language, about students' prior knowledge. Ms. Stern brought a reluctance to see the policy as something from which she could learn and so she did not learn. She continues to see it as duplication of what she already knows. Here are two teachers who started from similar places in thinking about reading and reading practices when they encountered the policy, yet who ended up learning different things from it.

Mr. Fielder brought a traditional view of reading to his learning from the policy, and anxiety over learning new ideas about reading. Yet he also brought his sense that the policy resonated with some familiar thoughts about his own reading processes. He knew, for instance, that when he read, if he already knew something about a topic it was easier for him to comprehend what he was reading. He also knew that what he knew influenced how he interpreted text. But before learning from the policy, Mr. Fielder never applied this understanding of his own reading to teaching children how to read. What he learned from the policy helped him do so. Even though Mr. Fielder brought traditional ideas about teaching and some fear of learning and change, he also brought a sense that the views of the policy were reasonable and helpful to him in teaching reading better.

Looking at what and how these teachers learned points out that they brought multifaceted and variegated baggage to their learning from the policy. Prior knowledge is not just what they "know," but who they are as learners, and what they believe. And among the three teachers, different ideas, beliefs, and dispositions took precedence over others in shaping the learning these teachers did. Even though these teachers shared some ideas, beliefs, and experiences (Ms. Stern's and Ms. Price's ideas about reading; Mr. Fielder's and Ms. Stern's reluctance to learn), the ideas did not all play the same role in shaping what and how the teachers learned. Ms. Price's and Ms. Stern's similarities in practices did not result in the same learning from the policy. Nor did Mr. Fielder's and Ms. Stern's resistance to change.

Much of what these stories point out is in line with cognitive views of learning. Learning is a process in which learners' schemata—their prior knowledge—affect what and how they learn. And when learning occurs, most often, new ideas are assimilated to fit into the learners' existing schemata (Bruner, 1983; Posner et al., 1983). Yet these stories add flesh to this very bony and linear description of learning. And, it seems, the flesh is what helps us understand how and what these teachers learned from this policy. These stories suggest that prior knowledge is actually an array of experiences, ideas, beliefs, and dispositions that form in unique ways when learners learn and therefore change, in unique ways, how and what they learn.

Ms. Price's case also points out that this array of ideas, beliefs, experiences, and so forth, does not remain the same. It changes, and therefore the learning learners do changes. Ms. Price continues to learn different ideas from the policy as she learns other new ideas and connects them to the policy. In connecting the ideas about student learning that she learned in the policy with ideas from conceptual-change instruction in science and "brain-based" learning, she made different sense than she originally did of what the reading policy was all about. In particular, she said she developed a new understanding of how students' prior knowledge influenced their reading comprehension. Her rethinking of the reading policy, in turn, helped her make different sense of the new ideas she encountered. The reading policy, when she "relearned" it, changed what she learned about conceptual change in science. So her story suggests that prior knowledge is not a one-way filter of new learning; it is shaped as well by new ideas that are learned. What Ms. Price "knew" changed as she learned and in turn changed what learning she did.

The teachers' stories suggest that their learning was a messy process in which *what* they learned varied because of this array of beliefs, ideas, and experiences called prior knowledge. This fits with the first view of learning in the beginning of the chapter—a reading of the policy as supporting a constructivist view of learning. These teachers seemed to do what policymakers thought they would do as learners—construct their own meaning of the policy.

These stories, however, suggest an additional complexity. Not only did these three teachers learn different things because of their prior knowledge and beliefs; they also constructed different opportunities to learn for themselves. Ms. Price and Mr. Fielder both attended the same in-service session on writing in which they were asked to write in a different way than they had in the past—a way the policy might support. The in-service presenter modeled a new kind of writing instruction in the session and allowed the participants to become learners of this new kind of instruction. Ms. Price learned a great deal from this experience. It spurred her to write more in her own life and to think differently about teaching writing in her classroom. Through this in-service experience and through her own writing, Ms. Price gained insight into what might be helpful to writers and what might hinder them. She used this insight to change how she taught writing to her students.

For Mr. Fielder, this experience meant very little. He never mentioned writing as a part of the policy, nor did he mention any changes in his writing instruction or his own writing because of what he learned. Mr. Fielder said he learned most from in-service sessions in which he could watch presenters model new activities, where he could see how he as a teacher should act in new ways. He did not use whatever he learned from the policy as a way to change his own reading or writing practices. For instance, Mr. Fielder did not talk about questioning himself more before he read a book, even though he now thought this was a useful thing to ask students to do before they read.

Like Mr. Fielder, Ms. Stern learned new ideas about reading and writing from a teacher's perspective—what teacher thinking and behavior the new ideas implied. She learned in her teacher education course such things as how she should set up a writer's workshop and how she should create a literate environment in her classroom. She did not relate what she learned about teaching reading and writing to her own reading and writing. For instance, she did not talk about using process writing to write her church bulletin, even though she thought process writing was important for her students as they learn to write. Although she learned new ideas about how to teach reading and writing, she had no experiences learning with these new ideas.

Ms. Price became a learner in these new ways, and Ms. Stern and Mr. Fielder did not. This difference in how they learned may have contributed to how these teachers made sense of the policy. Ms. Stern and Mr. Fielder talked about the policy (in Ms. Stern's case ideas associated with the policy) more in terms of how it changed what they did as teachers—new activities and strategies to use with their students—whereas Ms. Price talked about the policy as a changed approach to learning. Ms. Stern's and Mr. Fielder's sense-making of the policy rested on the assumption that if their teaching changed, so would their students' learning—learning as a reflection of teaching. Mr. Fielder and Ms. Price, though, are good examples of why this is a questionable assumption. They learned quite different things from what they were taught. Because Mr. Fielder and Ms. Stern did not experience the new ways of teaching as learners, it would have been difficult for them to understand how what they did as teachers played out for their learners and thus difficult to understand what might be necessary and important in order that their learners be able to learn in new ways.

Examples of staff-development efforts in which teachers have opportunities to become learners of new kinds of instruction are becoming more commonplace (e.g., the Bay Area Writer's Project, Marilyn Burn's mathematics workshops, SummerMath). The district in-service program that Ms. Price and Mr. Fielder attended had a few opportunities to do so. But Mr. Fielder's story points out that even when these opportunities are given, some teachers may not construct them as such. As teachers' arrays of ideas, beliefs, and experiences influence what they learn, they may also influence how they construct their opportunities to learn. This raises additional problems for those interested in helping teachers learn from policies. Even if state policymakers in this case could have figured out ways to help teachers in the state become learners in the new instructional ways of the policy, would all teachers have become learners? What would state policymakers have had to do to help teachers like Mr. Fielder see that understanding the policy from the learners' perspective might help him understand how to teach in new ways?

Furthermore, how could state policymakers help teachers learn to transfer the understandings they gained as learners to their teaching practices? Ms. Price, as a learner and teacher, was able to do this, but could all teachers? Lortie (1975) suggests that going to the other side of the desk (changing from learners to teachers) is a long-standing problem that beginning teachers face in learning to teach. Do experienced teachers learning to teach in new ways face the same problem?

If policymakers wanted teachers to learn about new ways of teaching reading from this policy, they would have had to figure out some answers to these kinds of questions. This study has been focusing on teachers' learning from policy and has only briefly mentioned that if teachers are learners from policy, then policymakers become teachers and as such face many of the same problems all teachers face. The irony of this story is that if the policy is to be believed, then the job of teacher becomes more difficult. If learners' prior knowledge shapes what and how they learn, how can teachers come to know the learners' prior knowledge and plan their teaching in light of it? Ms. Price struggles with this problem in her classroom, where she has ready access to her students and comes to know them well, but how could policymakers come to know their learners' prior knowledge when they teach them at a distance? How could policymakers as teachers come to understand the learning and change that their students have done?

FROM WHOSE PERSPECTIVE SHOULD WE COME TO UNDERSTAND CHANGE?

This study raises many questions about how we understand teachers' learning. If their learning is shaped by who they are and what they bring to learning, then teachers will learn different things from what they are taught and they will learn in different ways. So how do we think about what teachers have learned? Should their learning be measured as change or as an outcome?

If we are to understand learning from the learner's perspective, we need to understand where the learner started—this array of ideas, knowledge, beliefs, and experiences—and where they ended up after they learned. Learning from the learner's perspective is the distance they have traveled between what they knew, were, and believed and what they now know, are, and believe. From this perspective, Mr. Fielder has learned a great deal. As a result of what he learned from the policy, he has changed how he questions students and what texts he uses to teach reading Ms. Price has also traveled some distance because of the policy. She has changed her writing practices and her thinking about reading. Ms. Stern shows very little evidence of any changes directly related to the policy.

If, though, we are to understand learning from the policymakers' perspective, we must see learning as an outcome—something that is manifested in reading practices that resemble images of practice envisioned in their policy. Policymakers, like many teachers, measure learning by gauging how close learners seem to be to what they, as teachers, thought they taught. From this perspective, Ms. Stern has learned a great deal because her practices look similar to at least some readings of the policy. Mr. Fielder has learned little because his practices are still traditional, far away from most images of practices associated with the policy. That policymakers might understand learning from this perspective makes sense in that they believe they know the right way to teach reading and they want teachers to "know" it as well. Like many teachers, policymakers may want learning to be a reflection of their teaching—they want their learners to learn what as teachers they already know.

The stories of Mr. Fielder, Ms. Price, and Ms. Stern can be viewed either as successes or as failures for the reading policy depending on which perspective one chooses. Ms. Stern is a success to those looking for certain kinds of practices in classrooms, but a failure if looking for continued change and learning. Mr. Fielder is a successful learner, but policymakers may still question his practices. The purpose of outlining the two perspectives is not to decide which is right. Rather it is to raise the possibility that we may be able to learn something about policy making by looking at both perspectives.

WHAT CAN WE DO WITH UNDERSTANDING LEARNING FROM THESE TWO PERSPECTIVES?

The learners' perspective is critical to an understanding of how the policy has played out for these teachers and why. It helps show which parts of their arrays of ideas, knowledge, beliefs, and experiences interacted with the learning opportunities in order to help them learn and change. It helps us understand what makes learning difficult and what other kind of learning opportunities might be offered to make it less difficult. It helps us see where the policy may be weak, or just wrong, and where it is that teachers resist possible messages of the policy for good reasons. This perspective helps us see the genuine efforts to learn and change that teachers have made because of this policy. It also gives us an opportunity to learn from those genuine efforts so that we can understand how to bring about continued change and learning.

The policymaker's perspective on learning is a little more difficult to see value in, not because it is valueless but because its value has changed. In traditional policy studies, the policymaker's perspective was helpful in assessing which teachers were doing better and how much further every-one had to go. It assumed that there was a clear image of what teachers and students should be doing because of the policy, and therefore some way to measure how much more teachers had to learn to get it right. But, for the reading policy, there were few clear signals given to teachers about what the policy as enacted would look like. Furthermore, as the policy itself implies, policymakers all constructed different meanings of their ef-forts and so even if one policymaker put forth an image of exemplary practice, it is unlikely that others involved would agree. What reading should look like because of the policy continues to change and to be con-structed differently by different policymakers. This is not a deficiency in the policymakers' thinking. Images of the policy playing out in classrooms should change as policymakers and practitioners try out new ideas and become more thoughtful about what the ideas mean. It does, though, make it more difficult to use policymakers' perspectives as a benchmark to assess teachers' learning and actions. So what does this perspective have to offer if not a sense of how much more change teachers have to demonstrate in their practice?

What this perspective offers is a reminder that the ultimate goal of the policy was not to affect teacher learning, but to change how students learn to read in classrooms. Regardless of the lack of clarity and the changeable nature of what exactly the policy should look like in practice, it seems important to have a perspective on learning that looks beyond where teachers currently are. The value of this perspective is that it holds out a sense that there is a goal, albeit not a fixed one, to which teachers, as well as policymakers, must orient their continued change and learning.

WHAT ELSE MAY THESE STORIES SAY TO POLICYMAKERS?

Examining the implementation of the reading policy through stories of three teachers' learning opens up a different image or metaphor for policy implementation. These stories help us look at policy implementation as an incident of teaching and learning, rather than as a process by which ideas are filtered through the educational system and enacted by prac-titioners. The things we know about teaching and learning can help us understand how we might best look at a policy playing out in practice.

First, we must think of policy implementation not as a construction of output, but as a construction of change. This means that we cannot be fooled by policymakers or practitioners who espouse currently favored practices but who are not willing to continuously examine their ideas and practices and to evaluate them in light of new ideas. The measure of a teacher "doing" the policy should be determined not solely on how closely their practices resemble some set model of teaching, but on how open they are to learning, reflection, and change.

Second, we must think of policy implementation in the context of diverse and pluralistic learning styles of teachers. This means that learning opportunities that allow teachers to hear and think about policy ideas in multiple ways are critical. Some teachers, like Mr. Fielder, will learn best when given rather traditional staff-development opportunities, but other teachers, like Ms. Price, respond to opportunities that allow them to be more involved as learners. Some teachers, like Ms. Stern, may need opportunities that stress the dissonance between what they already know and the policy ideas in order for them to attend to the ideas at all. I have discussed only three teachers; the larger population is even more diverse. If policymakers want to engage teachers in policy ideas, they must do what all good teachers do, which is to provide multiple paths to get to the ideas.

Third, we must think of policy implementation as an exercise in teaching in the best sense. Policymakers' ideas may be a real improvement over current practices and policymakers may be better informed or more knowledgeable than practitioners about good and effective instruction. Policymakers may, occasionally at least, indeed know best. But we need to recognize that the measure of a policy's worth is not knowing the better way or even knowing better ways to teach teachers the better way. *The worth of a policy is in what teachers learn from it.* This means we must attend more to teachers' learning than to policymakers' actions. Regardless of the carefulness with which policymakers construct their ideas and construct the opportunities for teachers to learn the ideas, teachers will create their own learning of what they are taught. We must cultivate a genuine respect for the integrity of the learning process. This means attending to and learning from teachers' diverse interpretations of policy ideas as a way of getting smarter about how policy ideas might look in practice. At the same time, we must hold true to the ideas we want to introduce into practice. This means that as we attend to and learn from teachers' interpretation and enactment of policy ideas, we have to think about how to continue to teach in order to influence teachers' interpretations in fruitful ways.

Methodology and Research Procedures

In Chapter 1, I included a brief description of the methods of this study. In this appendix, I provide a more detailed description of the data collection and analysis.

SITE SELECTION

This study is part of a larger research project that has been looking at the relationship between state-level instructional policies and mathematics and reading instruction. In this project, researchers selected school districts that provided contrasting socioeconomic and demographic characteristics—socioeconomic status (SES), type of community (rural, suburban, urban), reputation of district, size—and in which district personnel were willing to participate in the study. The rationale for diversity among sites was that policies are likely to be attended to and played out differently in districts with varying economic, geographic, social, and political conditions (McLaughlin, 1987; Sproull, 1981).

TEACHER SELECTION

Within the schools selected for the larger project, I selected two teachers from the same site and one from another site. Choosing two teachers who shared the same teaching context and who experienced the same district policies and one teacher who differed allowed me to raise questions about the impact of context and district input on these three teachers' stories. For the larger project, researchers chose to look at second- and fifth-grade teachers so that they could explore differences that might exist between policy implementation in primary and intermediate grade levels. This seemed particularly important for a reading policy because primary grades have traditionally focused in reading instruction on teaching reading skills, whereas intermediate grades have been concerned with improving comprehension and fluency.

Within the selected sites and grade levels, I chose three teachers to study. My principal concern was finding teachers who were willing to be interviewed and observed for a two-year period. Teacher learning and change rarely occur quickly (Feiman-Nemser, 1983; Richardson, 1990). Thus, it was important to find teachers who were interested in participating for at least two school years.

I deliberately did not seek to select teachers who might be considered exemplary. I wanted to study teachers who, although not statistically representative, would not seem like outliers in the teaching population in the state. But figuring out the dimensions on which the teachers I studied should be similar to other teachers was difficult because little is known about what really influences teachers' learning. Do type of students, colleagues, years of experience, and so forth, shape how and what teachers learn? Because the dimensions of teacher learning were unclear, I looked instead for teachers who represented a range on dimensions important in teaching reading. These included such things as whether the teachers were considered "innovative" or "traditional" in their practices; whether they taught primary or intermediate level; what kind of students they had (SES, rural or urban, ability grouped or not, and so forth), and what, if any, their exposure to the policy had been. The three teachers I selected varied on these dimensions in the following ways:

1. Ms. Stern and Ms. Price were considered innovative by their principals; Mr. Fielder was considered a more traditional teacher.
2. Mr. Fielder and Ms. Stern taught second grade; Ms. Price taught fifth grade.
3. Mr. Fielder and Ms. Price had attended a workshop dedicated to the policy; Ms. Stern had not.
4. Mr. Fielder and Ms. Price worked in the same rural school with lower SES students; Ms. Stern worked in an affluent suburban school.
5. Ms. Stern and Mr. Fielder taught heterogeneously grouped students; Ms. Price taught students labeled "gifted underachievers."

In addition to varying on the above dimensions, these teachers also varied along other dimensions commonly considered important—age, years of teaching experience, kinds of teaching experiences, kinds of preservice education, and gender. Not all of these dimensions were, in the end, important in the study, but some were (such as preservice education and age) and so became useful areas in which to have contrasts. Second, for each dimension, there tended to be two teachers who were similar and one who was not. This meant that I could explore more subtle differences between two teachers who were similar along the dimension as well as differences between the pair more similar and the third teacher.

Having the teachers I selected vary along different dimensions seemed important not only for the opportunities it allowed me to investigate, but also for the appeal of these teachers' stories to a wider audience. Having teachers who have different types of reading practices, learning experiences, life circumstances, kinds of students, and so forth, may allow more policymakers, educational researchers, and teachers to see these three teachers' stories as familiar—stories that resonate with those of teachers they know and with whom they work.

Since this is an exploratory study, the sample of teachers I chose was not intended to offer generalizable findings about how Michigan teachers learned from the reading policy and, therefore, the sample is not representative of teachers in the state. However, *because* it is an exploratory study, the sample of teachers should vary to "facilitate the expansion of the developing theory" (Bogdan & Biklen, 1982, p. 67) of teacher learning from policy. Choosing three teachers rather than one teacher gave me the variance that seemed necessary. And, although more than three teachers would have introduced even greater variance, a larger number of teachers in the study would not have allowed me to interview and observe them as extensively as I did these three teachers. The trade-offs in this kind of work are always between breadth and depth and, although choosing two, four, five, or six teachers would be in any case arbitrary, the choice of three was consistent with the goals of the study and the limitations of research conducted by me as an individual investigator.

STATE- AND DISTRICT-LEVEL DATA

As part of the larger research project, researchers collected data from state-level informants, from district personnel, and from school principals about their own work in relationship to the policy, and to state and district procedures, policies, and practices in general. We used this information to gain an understanding of the context of the teachers as well as the learning opportunities related to the policy that may have been available to them. Along with one or two other project researchers, I interviewed state policymakers. Additionally, we interviewed teachers and district educators involved in designing state conferences on the policy and the Michigan Educational Assessment Program (MEAP) tests. District reading coordinators for both school districts represented were interviewed, as were both building principals. Finally, I read interviews of other teachers in both schools to check for additional perceptions of school policies and procedures.

In addition to interviewing state and district people, I attended one state and one district in-service program on literacy instruction to understand better the kinds of experiences that were available to the teachers. I wrote field notes for both in-service programs.

DATA COLLECTION

I collected data from the three teachers for a two-year period, during the 1990/1991 and 1991/1992 school years. For both the classroom observations and teacher interviews, I used a series of structured observation guidelines and interview protocols that I helped design for the larger research project. These instruments were designed to help focus data collection on what was assumed to be critical features of reading practice—use of text, discourse patterns, teaching of reading skills, and grouping of students; features of teacher learning—learning experiences connected to the policy, formal teacher education, informal learning opportunities; and finally features of knowledge of the policy—familiarity with policy and interpretation of policy. Many of the questions and focal areas in these instruments were drawn from interviews used in the Teacher Education and Learning to Teach study conducted by the National Center for Research on Teacher Education (MSU, 1986-1990) in which many of the researchers had been involved. These instruments were modified over the two-year period by project researchers when new areas of interest arose. Furthermore, I modified the interview protocols to allow me to probe more deeply into teachers' experiences with learning about the policy, learning to teach, and changes in their practices related to what they learned. For instance, during the second year of interviewing, I asked many additional questions about the teachers' own lives—such questions as where they lived, what their families were like, what they did in their spare time, where they went school, what they were like in elementary school, how they learned to read, and what, if at all, they read now as adults. These questions were important for me to gain a fuller picture of their lives as learners and how the context of their lives outside of school might influence their lives as teachers.

For each day of classroom observation, I took extensive field notes of the events of the day. What I chose to observe in the teachers' classrooms and what I chose to write about in my field notes were shaped by the analytic questions in the observation guide, as well as what appeared most salient to the teacher and students during the day I observed. Below is a sample of questions from the observation guide on discourse patterns in the literacy instruction:

> Reflect on the discourse patterns that you observed during the day. How did students participate? What kinds of things did students say, how much did they participate, what were they encouraged to do and not to do? Who talked? To whom? How were student ideas treated? What counted as legitimate talk? Was there press for convergence? Was there conversation in which no one right answer was guiding the discussion?

These analytic questions served as reminders of classroom occurrences for me to look for and note and therefore helped me approach the different classroom observations I did over a two-year period with some consistency.

After taking field notes in the classrooms, I "wrote up" each of my observations using the observation guide as a structure for my notes. These notes included narrative descriptions of the day's observation that ranged from 8–15 single-spaced pages in length. They also included answers to the analytic questions about reading practices in the guide. Again, these questions were on discourse during the lesson, special terminology used, student responses, student engagement, teacher assessment of students, and classroom atmosphere. I also taped and transcribed parts of the school day so that I could verify the exact discourse of the class in my notes. These second-level notes on my daily observations of teachers were most valuable in writing cases of the teachers. This first stage of analysis of the field notes I wrote in the classrooms helped me reflect *at the time* on what I observed. The reflection helped me raise questions to explore in future observations and interviews with the teachers. Using the structured observation guide helped me to write similar notes across the different observations for all three teachers.

For the interviews, I used three different interview protocols: the preobservation and post-observation protocols, each of which focused on the observation, and a long interview on the teachers' ideas, practices, and learning. The pre-observation interview focused on the teachers' planning and their expectation of what might occur during the day. The postobservation interview was extensive, focusing on what and how the teachers were trying to teach, what they thought had been accomplished, what they thought students might have learned, and how, if at all, they planned on following up the lesson. Additionally, I asked teachers where in their curriculum this lesson fit and whether the day was typical of their teaching.

The long interview centered on the following three areas:

1. *Teacher understanding of the reading policy.* The interview format included questions on teachers' awareness of the state efforts, their thinking about the new reading definition, their experiences with the policy (in-service work, conversation with peers, etc.), and the effects, if any, of the policy on their practices.
2. *Teachers' reading practices.* This section of the interview included questions on their reading practices in general—the purposes of reading instruction, what they see as important to teach, the pedagogy they see as appropriate, how they see reading relating to other subjects they teach. Additionally, it included questions about changes in their reading practices, both individual changes and changes at the school or district level such as new textbooks, new assessment measures, staff development programs, and so forth.
3. *Teacher learning.* The interview protocol included questions on where and how they learned to teach reading, both preservice and staff development. It also included questions about the teachers' informal learning experiences that may have contributed to their understanding of reading, as well as their personal reading habits.

The post-observation interviews lasted from 30 to 60 minutes. The long interview lasted from 90 minutes to two hours. I taped both of these interviews and transcribed the tapes. I did pre-observation interviews by telephone the night before or in person before the school day began and took notes of these interviews.

In addition to the formal interviews, I would converse with teachers during nonteaching times of the day—on the playground during recess duty, walking students to and from lunch or special area classes, at assemblies, or during class time when they were not teaching. I noted these conversations in my field notes and incorporated them into my notes of the day.

The nature of this kind of research is that it involves judgments on what data to collect and how to interpret it. My thinking about reading instruction, about teaching, and about the policy obviously influenced what I saw and heard and how I made sense of it. So to check in some way my judgments about the data, throughout the two year period of data collection, I asked other researchers to read my field notes and interviews. Other researchers' perspectives on my field notes and interviews helped to develop my thinking about these teachers' classroom practices and their talk about their own learning. And because other researchers read the data while I was still observing and interviewing these teachers, their comments helped me think about new features to look for in the teachers' reading practices and new questions to ask about their learning. Although obviously sharing my data with other researchers did not eliminate my biases entirely, it helped me see how others made sense of my data and I gained the benefit of others' perspectives on what I was collecting.

DATA ANALYSIS

Data collection and data analysis in this study were interactive over the two-year period. As mentioned earlier, the first step in analyzing the data was done during the time I observed the teachers as I wrote up notes of the observations. Writing up notes, reading transcribed interviews, and receiving other researchers' comments on my data prior to returning to observe and interview the teachers again helped refine what I looked for in practice next, so that the instruments did not remain static throughout the two years.

Analysis of Interview Data

The interview data included my notes of the pre-observation interviews and informal conversations, and transcriptions of taped post-observation and long teacher interviews. Because I talked with these teachers numerous times over the two year period, the data comprised a large data set. I organized the data both by person and by themes so that I could construct both individual cases of teachers and comparisons between the teachers.

As I read notes and the transcriptions of individual teacher interviews, I tagged the data around categories that were pertinent to my questions: What do the teachers say about their views of the policy? What are the teachers' reports about their learning? What changes in their reading practices do the teachers report? I then reconstructed the individual interview data into these categories and formulated possible answers to these questions. These answers helped me refine questions to ask the teachers in future interviews, which in turn helped me develop new categories around which to reconstruct my data. Thus I developed categories of analysis in an iterative process. For instance, for the first few teacher interviews, I created the category "view of reading and reading instruction." After I looked over comments from a few teacher interviews that pertained to this category, it became clear that the teachers said quite different things about what they thought reading was and what they thought reading instruction was. This became an interesting area to ask the teachers more questions about, and it became imperative that I set up two categories—view of reading and view of reading instruction—rather than one. After setting up new categories, I went back to previous interviews and pulled out additional comments pertaining to them.

I engaged in a similar process for all the teacher interviews and informal conversations and then combined the reconstructed interviews for each teacher. These combined reconstructed interviews served as the main body of interview data for the individual teacher case studies. The reconstructed interviews also made it easier for me to compare across teachers because the data for all three teachers were grouped in the same categories.

Analysis of Observation Data

The observation data primarily informed the interview data in that they provided a context in which to see the enactment of the teachers' statements. For instance, Ms. Stern described her reading practice as whole-language. She said that she integrates subject-area instruction around themes and always teaches skills going from the "whole to the part." Although these terms are commonplace in teaching circles, they mean very different things to different teachers. So my observation data collected in Ms. Stern's classroom helped me construct an image of what she meant by whole-language, moving from the whole to the part, and integrated subject-area instruction. Putting together her actions with her statements while I was still collecting data again allowed me to check my current hypotheses of what I was seeing and hearing and so refine my thinking about the teachers.

I separated the observation data into categories similar to the interview data. From the reconstructed versions of the interviews and observation data, I constructed the three case studies of these teachers and the chapter focused on comparisons of the teachers.

References

Anderson, R. (1984). Role of the reader's schema in comprehension, learning, and memory. In R. Anderson, J. Osborn, & R. Tierney (Eds.), *Learning to read in American schools: Basal readers and content texts* (pp. 243-257). Hillsdale, NJ: Erlbaum.

Anderson, R. C., Hiebert, E. H., Scott, J. A., & Wilkinson, I. A. G. (1985). *Becoming a nation of readers: The report of the Commission on Reading.* Washington, DC: National Institute of Education.

Anderson, R., Reynolds, R., Schallert, D., & Goetz, E. (1977). Frameworks for comprehending discourse. *American Educational Research Journal, 14,* 367-381.

Baier, V. E., March, J. G., & Saetren, H. (1988). Implementation and ambiguity. In J. G. March (Ed.), *Decisions and organizations* (pp. 150-164). Cambridge, MA: Basil Blackwell.

Blumer, H. (1976). The methodological position of symbolic interactionism. In M. Hammersly & P. Woods (Eds.), *The process of schooling: A sociological reader* (pp. 12-18). London: Routledge and Kegan Paul.

Bogdan, R., & Biklen, S. K. (1982). *Qualitative research for education: An introduction to theory and methods.* Boston: Allyn & Bacon.

Bowles, S., & Gintis, H. (1976). *Schooling in capitalist America: Educational reform and the contradictions of economic life.* New York: Basic Books.

Brown, R. G. (1991). *Schools of thought: How the politics of literacy shape thinking in the classroom.* San Francisco: Jossey-Bass.

Bruner, J. (1983). *In search of mind: Essays in autobiography.* New York: Harper & Row.

Bruner, J. (1990). *Acts of meaning.* Cambridge: Harvard University Press.

California State Department of Education. (1987). *Language arts framework.* Sacramento: Author.

Carter, K. (1990). Teachers' knowledge and learning to teach. In R. W. Houston (Ed.), *Handbook of research on teacher education* (pp. 291-310). New York: Macmillan.

Clandinin, D. J. (1985). Personal practical knowledge: A study of teachers' classroom images. *Curriculum Inquiry, 15,* 361-385.

Cohen, D. K. (1989). Teaching practice: Plus ça change. . . . In P. Jackson (Ed.), *Contributing to educational change: Perspectives on research and practice.* Berkeley, CA: McCutchan.

✳ ✳   Cohen, D. K., & Barnes, C. (1993). Policy as pedagogy. In D. K. Cohen, M. W. McLaughlin, & J. E. Talbert (Eds.), *Teaching for understanding: Challenges for policy and practice* (pp. 207-239). San Francisco: Jossey-Bass.

Cohen, M. D., March, J. D., & Olsen, J. P. (1972). A garbage can model of organizational choice. *Administrative Science Quarterly, 17,* 1-25.

Coles, R. (1989). *The call of stories: Teaching and the moral imagination.* Boston: Houghton Mifflin.

Delpit, L. (1988). The silenced dialogue: Power and pedagogy in educating other people's children. *Harvard Educational Review, 58,* 280-298.

Duckworth, E. R. (1987). *The having of wonderful ideas and other essays on teaching and learning.* New York: Teachers College Press.

Durkin, D. (1978-1979). What classroom observations reveal about reading comprehension instruction. *Reading Research Quarterly, 14,* 481-533.

Educational Evaluation and Policy Analysis. (1990). *12*(3), 233-353.

Elmore, R. F., & McLaughlin, M. W. (1988). *Steady work: Policy, practice, and the reform of American education.* Santa Monica, CA: Rand Corporation.

Feiman-Nemser, S. (1983). *Learning to teach* (Occasional Paper No. 64). East Lansing, MI: Institute for Research on Teaching.

✳ Firestone, W. A. (1989). Educational policy as an ecology of games. *Educational Researcher, 18*(7), 18-24.

Giroux, H. (1983). Theories of reproduction and resistance in the new sociology of education: A critical analysis. *Harvard Educational Review, 53,* 257-293.

Heath, S. B. (1982). What no bedtime story means: Narrative skills at home and school. *Language Society, 2,* 49-76.

Hollingsworth, S. (1989). Prior beliefs and cognitive change in learning to teach. *American Educational Research Journal, 26,* 28-36.

Jackson, P. (1986). *The practice of teaching.* New York: Teachers College Press.

Johnson, M. (1989). Personal practical knowledge series: Embodied knowledge. *Curriculum Inquiry, 19,* 361-377.

✳ Johnson, R. W., & O'Connor, R. E. (1979). Intraagency limitations on policy implementation: You can't always get what you want, but sometimes you get what you need. *Administration & Society, 11,* 193-211.

Kagan, D. M. (1992). Professional growth among preservice and beginning teachers. *Review of Educational Research, 62,* 129-169.

Keisler, S., & Sproull, L. (1982). Managerial response to changing environments: Perspectives on problem sensing from social cognition. *Administrative Science Quarterly, 27,* 548-570.

Kennedy, M. M. (1991). *An agenda for research on teacher learning* (National Center for Research on Teacher Learning Special Report). East Lansing: Michigan State University.

Kingdon, J. W. (1984). *Agendas, alternatives, and public policies.* Boston: Little, Brown.

Lampert, M. (1985). How do teachers manage to teach? Perspectives on problems in practice. *Harvard Educational Review, 55,* 178-194.

✳ Lieberman, A. (1982). Practice makes policy: The tensions of school improvement.

In A. Lieberman (Ed.), *Policymaking in education: Eighty-first yearbook of the National Society for the Study of Education. Part 1* (pp. 249-269). Chicago: University of Chicago Press.

Lipsky, M. (1980). *Street-level bureaucracy.* New York: Russell Sage Foundation.

Lively, P. (1984). *According to Mark: A novel.* New York: Beaufort Books.

Lortie, D. (1975). *Schoolteacher: A sociological study.* Chicago: University of Chicago Press.

McDonnell, L., & Elmore, R. (1987). Getting the job done: Alternative policy instruments. *Educational Evaluation and Policy Analysis, 9,* 133-152.

McLaughlin, M. W. (1987). Learning from experience: Lessons from policy implementation. *Educational Evaluation and Policy Analysis, 9,* 171-178.

McLaughlin, M. W. (1990). The Rand Change Agent Study revisited: Macro perspectives and micro realities. *Educational Researcher, 19*(9), 11-16.

Mead, G. H. (1934). *Mind, self and society.* Chicago: University of Chicago Press.

Meyer, J. W., & Rowan, B. (1978). The structure of educational organizations. In M. W. Meyer and Associates (Eds.), *Environments and organizations* (pp. 78-109). San Francisco: Jossey-Bass.

Michigan Reading Association. (1984). *Reading redefined: Michigan Reading Association position paper.* Lansing: Author.

Michigan State Board of Education. (1985). *Michigan essential goals and objectives for reading education.* Lansing: Author.

Michigan State Department of Education. (1987). *Reading at a glance for Michigan administrators.* Paper prepared for the Michigan Reading Association, Curriculum Review Committee, and Michigan State Board of Education.

Posner, G. J., Strike, K. A., Hewson, P. W., & Gertzog, W. A. (1983). Accommodation of a scientific conception: Toward a theory of conceptual change. *Science Education, 66,* 211-227.

Richardson, V. (1990). Significant and worthwhile change in teaching practice. *Educational Researcher, 19,* 10-18.

Rumelhart, D. E. (1980). Schemata: The building blocks of cognition. In R. J. Spiro, B. C. Bruce, & W. F. Brewer (Eds.), *Theoretical issues in reading comprehension: Perspectives from cognitive psychology, linguistics, artificial intelligence, and education* (pp. 33-58). Hillsdale, NJ: Erlbaum.

Sarason, S. (1982). *The culture of the school and the problem of change.* Boston: Allyn and Bacon.

Schwille, J., et al., (1983). Teachers as policy brokers in the content of elementary school mathematics. In L. Shulman & G. Sykes (Eds.), *Handbook of teaching and educational policy* (pp. 370-390). New York: Longman.

Shulman, L. S. (1987). Knowledge and teaching: Foundations of the new reform. *Harvard Educational Review, 57,* 1-22.

Sproull, L. (1981). Response to regulation: An organizational process framework. *Administration & Society, 12,* 447-470.

Weick, K. (1976). Educational organization as loosely coupled systems. *Administrative Science Quarterly, 21,* 1-19.

Weiss, J. A., & Cohen, D. K. (1991). *The interplay of social science and prior knowledge in policy and practice.* Unpublished paper prepared for a volume in honor of Charles E. Lindblom.

Willinsky, J. (1989). *The new literacy: Redefining reading and writing in the schools.* New York: Routledge.

Wilson, S. M., Shulman, L. S., & Richert, A. (1987). "150 different ways" of knowing: Representations of knowledge in teaching. In J. Calderhead (Ed.), *Exploring teachers' thinking* (pp. 104–124). London: Cassell.

Zukav, G. (1980). *The dancing Wu Li masters: An overview of the new physics.* New York: Bantam.

Index

About the Author

Nancy Jennings is an assistant professor in the education department at Bowdoin College in Brunswick, Maine. While a graduate student at Michigan State University, she worked with other researchers on the Educational Policy and Practice Study looking at the relationships between state curricular policies and classroom practice. Her research interests focus on teacher learning as well as the implementation of policies in schools serving traditionally disadvantaged students.